Sikkim General Knowledge
for SPSC Exams

Saurav Chettri
Copyright © 2025
All Rights Reserved

Forward

This is a short guidebook on Sikkim General Knowledge, specifically tailored for the Sikkim Public Service Commission (SPSC) exams. The content is a compilation of my own notes, which proved instrumental in my success in cracking the SPSC exam. The scarcity of information on Sikkim GK necessitated the publication of this concise guide to assist aspiring candidates.

I've tried to keep the book strictly on Sikkim GK only, so as to make it concise yet effective to save your time in preparing the Sikkim GK part. However, I've included few other topics, especially information on superlatives and important organizations of the world. In addition, the book contains over 200 important Sikkim GK questions that are generally asked in the SPSC Exams.

Wishing you the best of luck in your preparations.

Contents

Sikkim Info 1

    Rivers of Sikkim 3

    Mountain Passes 4

    Mountain Ranges in Sikkim 5

    Lakes 5

    Dams 5

    Wildlife Sanctuaries 7

History Of Sikkim 9

    Chogyals Of Sikkim 10

Sikkim State Leadership (As of Feb 2025) 28

First in Sikkim 30

Festivals of Sikkim 32

    Music & Dance of Sikkim 36

Sikkim Award Winners 39

Buddhism 40

    Schools of Tibetan Buddhism 40

    Monastries in Sikkim 41

North Eastern Council 43

UN & Other Important World Organizations 44

    The United Nations 44

    International Organizations 48

    Sports Federations 53

    International Summits & Conferences 53

Flora & Fauna of India 56

    Biosphere reserves 57

Superlatives 58

    Important Superlatives of India 58

    List of First in India 60

    Awards and Honours 63

    List of First in World 64

Sikkim General Knowledge Question Bank 66

Sikkim Info

- **Admission to India** – 16 May 1975
- **Area - 7096 sq. km** (2nd smallest state, after Goa)
- **Altitude** ranges from **300m to 8,586m** above sea level
- **Gangtok is at an elevation of 1,650 m** (5,410 ft) (1m = 3.28 ft)
- **Population - 6.10 Lakhs** (Least Populated State in the Country) (2011 Census)
- **Male Population - 321,661 (**2011 Census)
- **Female Population - 286,027** (2011 Census)
- **First Census** of Sikkim was conducted in the year **1891**
- **Population Density - 86/sq. km** (3rd lowest state in terms of population density) (2011 Census)
- **Official Languages** -English, Nepali, Sikkimese (Bhutia) and Lepcha **(4)**. Additional official languages include Gurung, Limbu, Magar, Mukhia, Newari, Rai, Sherpa and Tamang for the purpose of preservation of culture and tradition in the state. (12 languages)
- **Mean annual rainfall** varies from **2000 mm. to 4000 mm**
- **Sex Ratio - 890** females for every 1000 males (2011 Census)
- **Child Sex Ratio – 944** (2011 Census)
- **International Borders -** China on North, Nepal on West & Bhutan on East
- **Area under State Forest Department - 5841 sq. km (82.31% area)** (2019)
- **Total Forest Cover - 3342.49 sq. km (47.11 %)** (2019)
- **State Animal - Red panda** (Listed as **Endangered** in the IUCN red list of Threatened Species and under Schedule I of the Indian Wildlife (Protection) Act, 1972, the red panda has the highest legal protection at par with other threatened species.)
- **State Tree - Rhododendron niveum**
- **State Flower - Dendrobium Nobile (Noble Orchid)**
- **State Bird - Blood Pheasant**
- **State Fish - Copper Mahseer** (Katley)
- **Literacy Rate - 82.2% (13th)** (2011 Census)
- **Male Literacy Rate - 87.29 %** (2011 Census)
- **Female Literacy Rate - 76.43 %** (2011 Census)
- **Urban Population - 24.97%** people live in urban regions.
- **Suicide rate - 43.1 (per 100,000 population,** 2022 NCRB data) (1st in states of India) (National Average - 12.4)
- **GDP – Rs. 52,555 crore** (2024-25 estimate)
- **GDP per capita - 587,743** (highest in India) (2023-24)

- **Khangchendzonga National Park - UNESCO World Heritage Site** (2016) (35% Area covered by it)
- Sikkim is located in the **high-risk seismic zone IV** of the Indian seismic zoning map.

Figure 1- Map of Sikkim

<u>Rivers of Sikkim</u>

1. **Teesta**
- Origin - Cholamu Lake, Zemu Glacier, North Sikkim
- Length - 315 km
- Tributaries:
- Left Tributaries - Dik Chhu, Rangpo River, Lang Chu, Lachung River, Rani Khola
- Right Tributaries - Ranghap Chhu, Rangeet, Ringyong Chhu
- Mouth - Brahmaputra River (Fulchhari, Gaibandhu, Bangladesh)

2. **Rangeet**
- Origin - Rathong Glacier, West Sikkim
- Rangit River meets the Teesta River at a confluence known as Triveni, which is located near the border of Sikkim with West Bengal

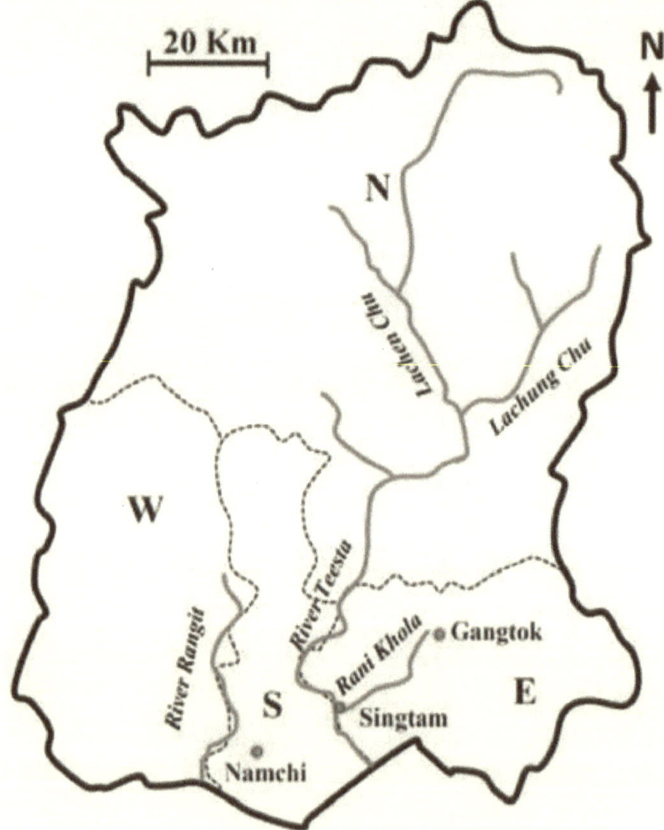

Figure 2- Major Rivers of Sikkim

Mountain Passes

1. **Nathula Pass**
   - Connects India & Tibet
   - Is in East Sikkim at a height of 14140 ft (4,310m) above sea level.

2. **Jelep La Pass**
   - India – Tibet
   - East Sikkim
   - At an elevation of 4267m

3. **Donkia Pass**
   - Between Lachen and Lachung Valleys
   - North Sikkim
   - 5,500m above sea level

4. **Chiwabhanjyang Pass**
   - Nepal – Sikkim
   - West Sikkim
   - 3,139m above sea level

Figure 3 - Major Passes of Sikkim

Mountain Ranges in Sikkim

Singalila Ridge
- The **Singalila Ridge** is a north-south mountain ridge running from northwestern West Bengal through Sikkim in the Indian part of the Himalayas. The district of Ilam in Nepal falls on the western part of this ridge.
- The ridge separates mountain ranges of West Bengal from other Himalayan ranges to its west. The two highest peaks of West Bengal, **Sandakphu** (3,636 m (11,929 ft)) and Phalut (3,600 m (11,800 ft)) are located on the ridge.

Dongkya Range
- **Dongkya Range** is a mountain range in the lower Himalayas that forms the **eastern** border of Sikkim. Its northern tip extends to Dongkha La, and as it moves southwards, it is cut by Cho La, Yak La, Nathu La and Jelep La passes.
- It was established as the border between Sikkim and Tibet's Chumbi Valley by the **1890 Convention of Calcutta** reached between British India and Qing China.

Lakes

1. **Tsomgo Lake** - East Sikkim (About 40kms from Gangtok)
2. **Cholamu Lake** - North Sikkim (Highest Lake in India at an altitude of 5,100m/ 16700 ft)
3. **Gurudongmar Lake** - North Sikkim
4. **Khecheopalri Lake** - West Sikkim

Dams

1. **Teesta -V (NHPC) Dam** - Teesta River, Dikchu, Gangtok District (Length - 176.5m. Height - 86.8m). Output – 510MW
2. **Teesta – III (Teesta Urja)** – Chungthang, Mangan District (Length – 298m. Height -60m). On 4 October, 2023 heavy rains caused a glacial lake outburst flood which destroyed this dam. Output – 1200MW.
3. **Rangit III Dam** - Rangit River, Legship, Gyalshing District (Length - 105m. Height - 45m). Output – 60MW.

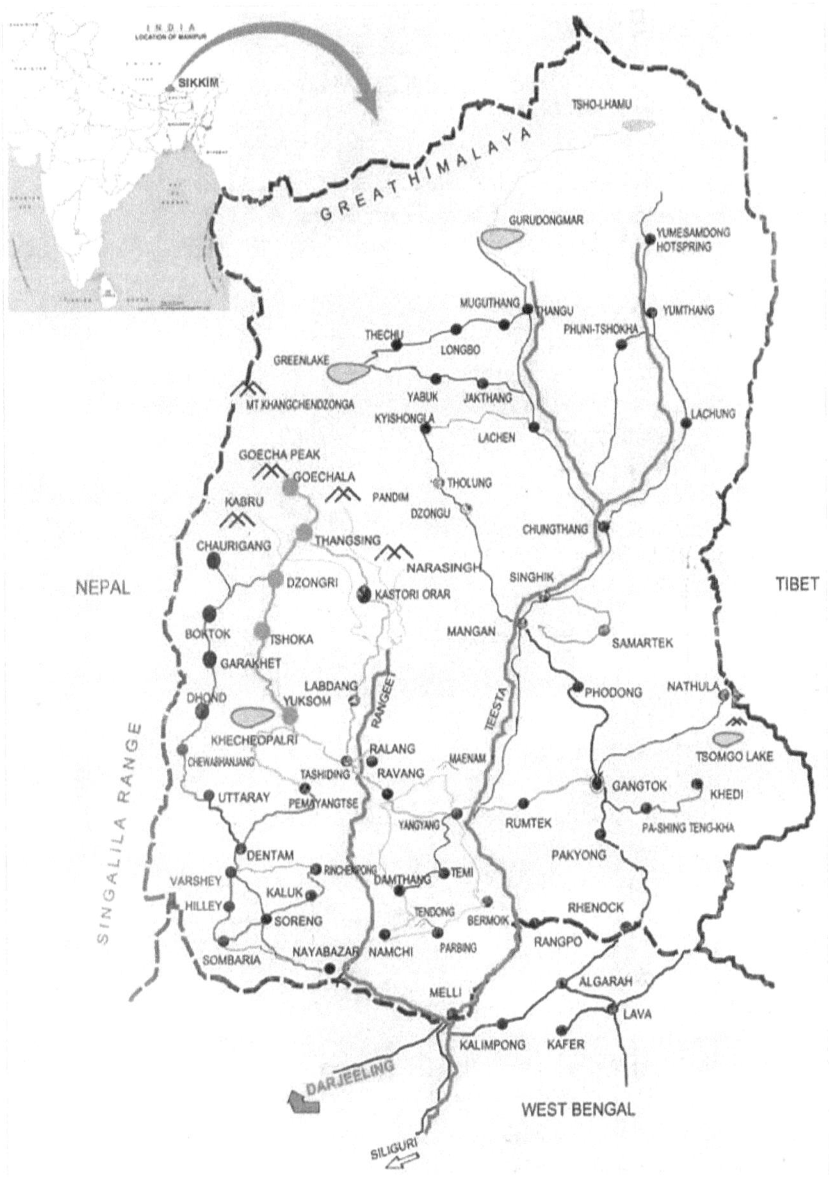

Figure 4- Major Lakes & Mountains of Sikkim

<u>**Wildlife Sanctuaries**</u>

1. **Barsey Rhododendron Wildlife Sanctuary**
   - Soreng District
   - Area - 104 sq. km
   - Surrounded by the Singalila Range and borders Nepal on the West
   - Rhododendron bloom during March & April

2. **Pangolakha Wildlife Sanctuary**
   - Pakyong District
   - 128 sq. km
   - Home to Asiatic Black Bear, Red Fox and about 300 Red Pandas which also happens to be the largest number in the world reserved at one place.
   - Wide varieties of exotic birds

3. **Fambong Lho Wildlife Sanctuary**
   - Gangtok District
   - 52 sq. km
   - Regarded as extension of Kanchendzonga National Park.

4. **Kyongnosla Alpine Wildlife Sanctuary**
   - Gangtok District
   - 31 sq. km

5. **Shingba Rhododendron Sanctuary**
   - Mangan District
   - 43 sq km
   - Located in Yumthang Valley of Flowers, north of Lachung

6. **Maenam Wildlife Sanctuary**
   - Namchi District
   - 36 sq km
   - Literal meaning of Maenam is - "Treasure house of medicines"

7. **Kitam Bird Sanctuary**
   - Namchi District
   - 6 sq km

<u>**Kanchendzonga National Park**</u>
   - North and West Sikkim
   - 1784 sq. km
   - Has Mount Kanchendzonga (8586m), highest peak in India & third highest in the World

- UNESCO World Heritage Site (July 2016)
- It was included in the UNESCO Man and Biosphere (MAB) Programme in 2018.

WILDLIFE PROTECTED AREAS IN SIKKIM

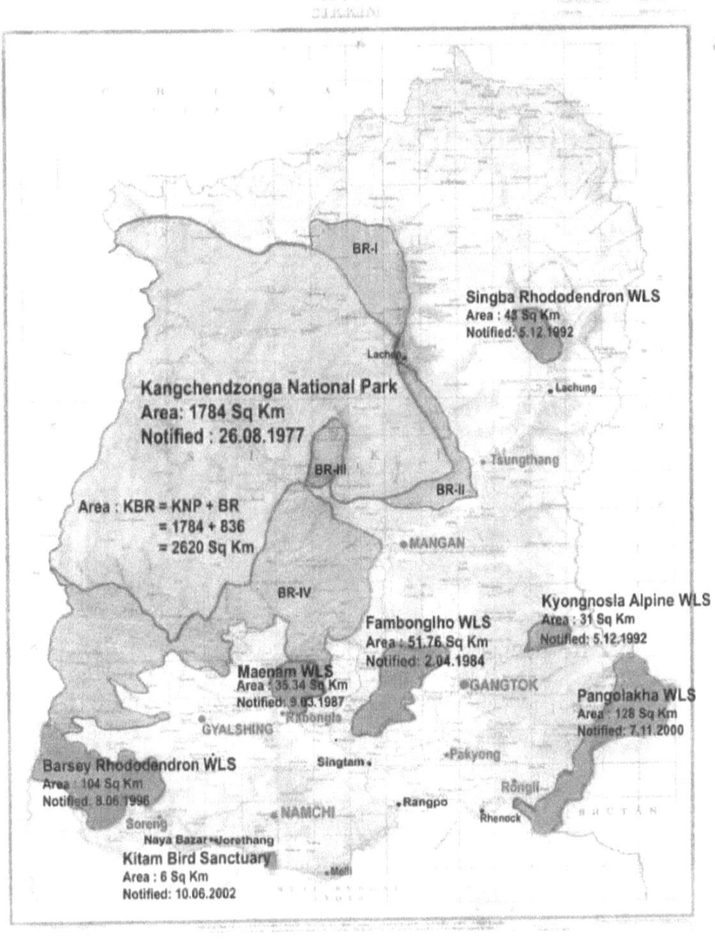

Note –

- Area of Kangchendzonga National Park (KNP) = **1784 sq km**
- Area of Buffer Region (BR) = **836 sq km**
- Total area of Kangchendzonga Biosphere Reserve (KBR) = **1784 + 836 = 2620 sq km**

History Of Sikkim

Ancient History of Sikkim: Pre-Chogyal Era

1. Limited Historical Records
- Sikkim's ancient history remains largely undocumented, relying on oral traditions, folklore, and scattered references in Tibetan and Indian texts.

2. Indigenous Inhabitants
- The **Lepchas** are believed to be the earliest settlers of Sikkim, practicing animism and living in harmony with nature.
- Dr. A. C. Singh in his work 'Population of Sikkim: A Geographical Analysis' (1983) mentions that Sikkim was home to the **Kirati tribes** from prehistoric times.

3. Hindu Mythological Connections
- According to Hindu mythology, Lord Shiva appeared as **Kirateshwar (Lord of the Kiratas)** to Arjuna at the site of the present Kirateshwar Mahadev Temple in Legship, West Sikkim.

4. Buddhist Influence
- In the 9th century, **Guru Rinpoche (Padmasambhava)** is believed to have passed through Sikkim.
- He blessed the land, introduced Buddhism, and prophesied the establishment of a Buddhist monarchy in the region, which materialized centuries later.

Formation of the Chogyal Dynasty

1. Guru Tashi's Journey to Denzong (13th Century)
- Guru Tashi, a prince of the Minyang Dynasty of Tibet, had a divine vision instructing him to seek his fortune in the "Denzong" (Valley of Rice)—the land now known as Sikkim.
- Following this vision, he and his followers migrated southward.

2. Khye Bumsa and the Lepcha Alliance
- After Guru Tashi's death, his elder son Khye Bumsa settled in Chumbi Valley (modern-day Tibet).
- He established contact with Lepcha chieftain Thekong Tek, a respected religious leader in Gangtok.
- Prophecy of Rule: Thekong Tek blessed Khye Bumsa, foretelling that his descendants would rule Sikkim.
- Their relationship strengthened over time, culminating in the **Treaty of Brotherhood at Kabi Longtsok**, symbolizing unity between the Bhutias and Lepchas.

3. Succession and Rise of Guru Tashi
Line of Succession:
- Khye Bumsa → Mipon Rab → Guru Tashi (fourth son of Mipon Rab).
- Guru Tashi moved to Gangtok and assumed leadership.
- After Thekong Tek's death, the Lepchas sought protection and leadership under Guru Tashi.
- He appointed a Lepcha chief advisor, further solidifying Bhutia-Lepcha ties.

4. Guru Tashi: The First Ruler of Sikkim
- Guru Tashi became the first ruler of Sikkim.
- His descendants would eventually establish a Buddhist monarchy, culminating in the coronation of Phuntsog Namgyal as the first Chogyal in 1642.

Chogyals Of Sikkim

- Ruled from 1642-1975, **around 333 years.**

Namgyal Dynasty

1. Phuntsok Namgyal
- Born 1604 - died 1670
- Ruled from 1642 -1670
- Phuntsog Namgyal was the **founder of the Namgyal dynasty** and the **first Chogyal (Dharma King) of Sikkim**. He was consecrated in **1642 at Yuksom** by three great lamas, fulfilling an ancient prophecy of Guru Padmasambhava (Guru Rinpoche). His reign marked the **foundation of Sikkim as a Buddhist kingdom**, laying the religious, political, and administrative framework that shaped Sikkim's history for centuries.

Early Life & The Prophecy
- Born in 1604, he was the son of Guru Tenzing and the great-grandson of Guru Tashi, a noble from the Minyak House of Kham, Tibet, who had migrated to Sikkim in the 13th century.
- Guru Rinpoche's Prophecy: In the 9th century, Guru Rinpoche prophesied that a "Phuntsok from the East" would become the ruler of a Buddhist kingdom in the Himalayas.
- In 1642, three powerful lamas—Lhatsun Chhenpo (North), Nga-dag Lama (West), and Kathhog Lama (South)—searched for the prophesied king and found Phuntsog Namgyal in present-day Gangtok.

Coronation & Establishment of the Namgyal Dynasty (1642)
- He was crowned in Norbughang, Yuksom by the three lamas, marking the beginning of the Chogyal monarchy.
- **Yuksom became the first capital** of Sikkim.
- The three lamas performed Buddhist rituals and established Mahayana Buddhism as the state religion.

Political & Administrative Achievements
1. **Territorial Expansion**
   - Expanded the kingdom to include:
     - Chumbi Valley (Tibet)
     - Parts of present-day Darjeeling (India)
     - Parts of eastern Nepal
   - His rule covered a much larger area than present-day Sikkim.
2. **Centralized Governance**
   - Divided the kingdom into 12 districts (Dzongs), each ruled by a Lepcha Dzongpon (Governor).
   - Established a Council of 12 Ministers to assist in administration.
3. **Religious & Cultural Integration**
   - Promoted Mahayana Buddhism, integrating Lepcha, Bhutia, and Tibetan traditions into Sikkim's culture.

Legacy
1. **Founder of the Kingdom of Sikkim**
   - Established a lasting monarchy that ruled until Sikkim's merger with India in 1975.
2. **Patron of Buddhism & Religious Harmony**
   - Laid the spiritual and cultural foundations of Sikkim as a Buddhist kingdom.
3. **Administrative Reforms**
   - Introduced centralized governance and district administration.
4. **Historical Importance**
   - His rule is seen as the beginning of modern Sikkimese identity.
   - Yuksom, his coronation site, is still a sacred place for Sikkimese Buddhists today.

2. <u>Tensung Namgyal</u>

- Born 1644- Died 1717
- Ruled from 1670-1700
- Tensung Namgyal was the second Chogyal (King) of Sikkim, ruling from 1670 to 1700. He was the son of Phuntsog Namgyal, the founder of the Namgyal dynasty. His reign was marked by political consolidation, the shift of the capital to Rabdentse, and the continuation of Buddhist governance in Sikkim.

Shift of Capital from Yuksom to Rabdentse (1670s)

- Moved Sikkim's capital from Yuksom to Rabdentse, near present-day Pelling.
- Rabdentse became the political and cultural center of Sikkim for over 100 years (1670–1793).
- The ruins of Rabdentse remain an important historical site today.

Strengthening the Monarchy & Administration

- Consolidated his father's reforms and maintained a strong centralized administration.

- Continued the system of 12 Dzongs (districts), governed by Lepcha and Bhutia officials.

Marital Alliances & Diplomacy

- Strengthened ties with Tibet and Bhutan through marriages with Tibetan and Bhutanese princesses.
- This helped secure Tibetan support against external threats.
- Had three wives from Bhutan, Tibet and a Limbu Princess.
- Built a new palace and asked his Limbu wife to name it. She named it "Song Khim" which in Limbu language means "New Palace".

Religious & Cultural Patronage

- Promoted Buddhism as the state religion, continuing his father's legacy.
- Encouraged the construction of monasteries and religious institutions.

External Threats & Conflicts

- Faced challenges from neighbouring Bhutan and Nepal.
- Maintained diplomatic relations with Tibet to safeguard Sikkim's independence.

3. <u>Chakdor Namgyal</u>

- Born 1686 - Died 1717
- Ruled from 1700-1717
- Chakdor Namgyal, the third Chogyal of Sikkim (1700–1717), had one of the most turbulent reigns in Sikkimese history. His rule was marked by internal succession disputes, a Bhutanese invasion, Tibetan intervention, and significant religious reforms.

Succession Dispute with Half-Sister Pediongmu

- Chakdor Namgyal was son of Tensung Namgyal from his second wife.
- Chakdor Namgyal's half-sister Pediongmu (daughter of the first wife of Tensung Namgyal) challenged his claim to the throne.
- Pediongmu allied with Bhutan, leading to a Bhutanese invasion of Sikkim.

Bhutanese Invasion & Exile to Tibet

- Bhutanese forces captured Rabdentse Palace, Sikkim's capital.
- They imprisoned the son of Yungthing Yeshe, Chakdor Namgyal's loyal minister.
- With Yungthing Yeshe's help, Chakdor Namgyal escaped to Lhasa, Tibet.

Life in Tibet & Tibetan Intervention

- Became a distinguished scholar and was appointed State Astrologer to the 6th Dalai Lama.
- The Tibetan government intervened, forcing the Bhutanese King (Deb Raja) to withdraw from Sikkim.
- Returned to Sikkim and successfully expelled the remaining Bhutanese forces.

- However, southern territories like Kalimpong remained under Bhutanese control.

Religious & Administrative Reforms

- Issued a **royal decree** requiring the second of every three sons of a Bhutia family to become a monk at **Pemayangtse Monastery.**
- Built **Guru Lhakhang in Tashiding (1715),** an important religious structure.

Assassination by Pediongmu

- Pediongmu conspired with a Tibetan doctor, who secretly opened Chakdor Namgyal's main artery while he was holidaying in Ralang hot springs, causing his death due to blood loss.
- Pediongmu was executed by strangulation with a silk scarf.
- The Tibetan doctor was executed at Namchi as punishment.

4. <u>Gyurmed Namgyal</u>

- Born 1707- Died 1733
- Ruled from 1717-1733
- Gyurmed Namgyal, the fourth Chogyal of Sikkim (1717–1733), ruled during one of the most unstable periods in Sikkimese history, facing Bhutanese invasions, territorial losses, internal revolts, and a controversial succession claim. His **untimely death at 26** left Sikkim without a strong ruler, leading to further political crises.

Accession & Political Struggles (1717)

- Son of Chakdor Namgyal, he ascended the throne after his father's assassination.
- His rule was dominated by court factions, and nobles manipulated governance.

Bhutanese Invasions & Border Disputes

- Bhutan still controlled parts of southeastern Sikkim (Kalimpong region).
- Frequent boundary conflicts with Bhutan weakened Sikkim's authority.
- Tibet remained Sikkim's key ally, intervening in major disputes.

Fear of Gurkha Invasion & Forced Labor

- The growing power of the Gorkhas (Nepal) threatened Sikkim's western borders.
- Ordered the fortification of Rabdentse Palace, forcing the local population into labor.
- This led to resentment among the Limbus (Tsongs), sparking revolts.

Revolt & Loss of Limbuana to Nepal

- Many Limbus rebelled against forced labor and fled to Nepal, forming a rebel district called Limbuana.
- Limbuana was permanently lost to Nepal, reducing Sikkim's western territories.

Controversial Succession & Death (1733)
- Died at the young age of 26 under mysterious circumstances.
- On his deathbed, he claimed that a nun from Sanga Choeling Monastery (near Pelling) was pregnant with his child.
- Many disbelieved the claim, as he was rumored to be impotent.
- The supposed child later became **Phuntsok Namgyal II, the fifth Chogyal of Sikkim**.

5. <u>Phuntsok Namgyal II</u>
- Born 1733 - Died 1780
- Ruled from 1733-1780
- Phuntsok Namgyal II, the fifth Chogyal of Sikkim (1733–1780), ruled during a time of political instability, external invasions, and Tibetan influence. His succession was controversial, as many doubted his legitimacy due to the circumstances of his birth. His reign was dominated by prolonged Bhutanese aggression and Sikkim's increasing dependence on Tibet for protection.

Controversial Succession & Tibetan Support
- Alleged son of Gyurmed Namgyal and a Buddhist nun from Sanga Choeling Monastery.
- Many nobles and factions questioned his legitimacy, as Gyurmed Namgyal was rumored to be impotent.
- Tibet, which had a strong influence over Sikkim, supported his claim to the throne.

Long Period of Interregnum (1733–1737)
- After Gyurmed Namgyal's death, Sikkim had no ruler for almost four years due to internal disputes.
- The Tibetan authorities finally intervened in 1737 and appointed Phuntsok Namgyal II as Chogyal.

Bhutanese Aggression & Territorial Losses
- Bhutan repeatedly invaded Sikkim, taking advantage of the kingdom's internal weaknesses.
- Sikkim increasingly relied on Tibet for military and diplomatic support.

Religious & Administrative Developments
- Continued to support Buddhism, reinforcing Tibetan influence over Sikkimese culture.
- Faced difficulty in governance due to power struggles among nobles and monks.

Later Years & Death (1780)
- His reign ended in 1780, after nearly five decades of rule.
- Succeeded by Tenzing Namgyal (6th Chogyal of Sikkim).

6. <u>**Tenzing Namgyal**</u>
- Born 1769-Died 1793, aged 24
- Ruled from 1780-1793
- Tenzing Namgyal, the sixth Chogyal of Sikkim (1780–1793), ruled during a time of territorial losses, rising Nepalese power, and exile to Tibet. His reign marked one of the darkest periods in Sikkimese history, as the kingdom lost large portions of its land to Nepal (Gorkhas) and Bhutan.

Continued Bhutanese & Gorkha Invasions
- Sikkim had already lost parts of southeastern territories (Kalimpong) to Bhutan during his father's rule.
- The Gorkhas of Nepal launched multiple attacks, seizing large parts of western Sikkim.
- Bhutan expanded its control in the south, while Nepal pushed into the west.

Major Territorial Losses to Nepal (1780)
- Gorkhas invaded western Sikkim, capturing Ilam, and Limbuana (now part of Nepal).
- This was a permanent loss, as these regions were later fully integrated into Nepal.

Exile to Tibet (1788)
- Nepalese attacked Rabdentse and Tenzing Namgyal fled to Tibet.
- He sought military help from the Qing Dynasty (China), which controlled Tibet.
- However, Tibet and China did not provide direct military assistance, leaving Sikkim in crisis.

The Sino-Nepalese War & Nepal's Withdrawal (1792)
- In 1788 and 1791, Nepal launched invasions into Tibet, attacking monasteries and trade centers.
- This provoked China's intervention, leading to the Sino-Nepalese War (1788–1792).
- The Chinese and Tibetan armies defeated the Gorkhas, forcing them to withdraw from Sikkim in 1792.
- However, Sikkim's lost western territories were not restored, and Nepal retained control over them.

Treaty of Titalia & Further Territorial Adjustments (1817)
- Though Tenzing Namgyal died in 1793, his reign set the stage for the 1817 Treaty of Titalia between Sikkim and the British.
- The treaty returned some lands to Sikkim, establishing the modern Nepal-Sikkim border.
- Additionally, Sikkim ceded the Chumbi Valley to Tibet, though the Sikkimese retained estates there.

Death & Succession (1793)
- Died in exile in Tibet in 1793.

- His son, Tshudpud Namgyal (7th Chogyal of Sikkim), succeeded him.

7. <u>Tsugphud Namgyal</u>

- Born 1785-Died 1863
- Ruled from 1793 - 1863
- Tshudpud Namgyal, the **seventh and longest-serving Chogyal** of Sikkim (1793–1863), ruled during a time of major geopolitical changes, British intervention, and territorial disputes. His reign saw the Anglo-Nepalese War (1814–1816), the Treaty of Titalia (1817), the permanent loss of Darjeeling (1835), and eventual British military action against Sikkim (1850 & 1861).

Shift of Capital to Tumlong

- Rabdentse was too close to the Nepalese border, making it vulnerable to attacks.
- He moved the capital to Tumlong, near Mangan, for better security.

Anglo-Nepalese War (1814–1816) & Treaty of Sugauli

- Sikkim allied with British India against Nepal.
- The Gorkha Empire had expanded aggressively, annexing Sikkim, Kumaon, and Garhwal.
- In 1814, the British and Nepal went to war, which ended with Nepal's defeat in 1816.
- **Treaty of Sugauli (1815–1816):**
  - Treaty of Saugali was signed by East India Company and King of Nepal in 2 December 1815 and ratified by 4 March 1816
  - Nepal was forced to give up its annexed territories, including Sikkim in the east and Kumaon & Garhwal in the west.

Treaty of Titalia (1817) – British Recognize Sikkim's Sovereignty

- In 1817, Tshudpud Namgyal signed the Treaty of Titalia with the British East India Company.
- **Key Provisions:**
  - The British restored Sikkim's lands annexed by Nepal.
  - In return, the British gained trading rights and passage up to the Tibet frontier.
  - The Sikkim-Nepal boundary was officially established along the Mahanadi and Mechi rivers and the Singalila mountain range.

Gifted Darjeeling (1835)

- In 1835, Tshudpud Namgyal gifted Darjeeling to the British for an annual subsidy fee.
- The British never paid the agreed compensation, leading to worsening relations.

British-Sikkim Conflict (1849–1850) – Military Attacks & Annexation

- In 1849, Sikkimese authorities arrested Joseph Hooker (a British botanist) and A. Campbell (the Superintendent of Darjeeling).

- The British saw this as an act of defiance and launched two military attacks in 1850 and 1861.
- In 1850, the British retaliated by annexing the Terai region (now part of present-day Kalimpong).

Treaty of Tumlong (1861) – Sikkim Becomes a British Protectorate

- After the British military action in 1861, Tshudpud Namgyal lost control of Sikkim's governance.
- His son, Sidkeong Namgyal, was made partial ruler (Raja) of Sikkim in 1861.
- **Treaty of Tumlong (1861):**
    - Signed in March 1861 between Great Britain and Kingdom of Sikkim, signed by Chogyal Sidkeong Namgyal.
    - Guaranteed free trade and protection for British travelers in Sikkim.
    - Sikkim became a de facto British protectorate, losing much of its autonomy.

Later Years & Death (1863)

- Tshudpud Namgyal ruled for almost 70 years, making him the longest-serving Chogyal of Sikkim.
- Died in 1863, and his son Sidkeong Namgyal (8th Chogyal) fully took over.

8. <u>**Sidkeong Namgyal**</u>

- Born 1819-Died 1874
- Ruled from 1863-1874
- Sidkeong Namgyal, the eighth Chogyal of Sikkim (1863–1874), ruled during a period of British dominance, political instability, and continued loss of Sikkimese autonomy. His reign was largely influenced by the British, who had effectively turned Sikkim into a protectorate following the Treaty of Tumlong (1861).

Treaty of Tumlong & British Control (1861)

- The **Treaty of Tumlong (1861)**, which was signed during his father's reign, remained in effect:
    - Allowed free trade and British control over external affairs.
    - Guaranteed British protection for travellers in Sikkim.
    - Further weakened the monarchy, making Sikkim a de facto British protectorate.

British Payment for Darjeeling (1850–1874)

- The British started paying an annual subsidy of Rs. 6,000 in 1850 for Darjeeling, which had been gifted to British in 1835.
- Later, this subsidy was increased to Rs. 12,000 per annum.
- This payment was not a compensation but an annual tribute to maintain British control.

Increasing British Influence & Loss of Autonomy
- The British now had direct influence over Sikkim's administration.
- British policies were implemented through indirect control, rather than direct governance.
- The Chogyal was mostly reduced to a symbolic ruler, while actual power shifted to the British.

Tensions with Tibetan Monasteries & Internal Struggles
- Many Buddhist monasteries in Sikkim still maintained strong Tibetan influence.
- The British wanted to reduce Tibetan control, leading to conflicts between pro-Tibet and pro-British factions in Sikkim.

9. <u>**Thutob Namgyal**</u>
- Born 1860-Died 1914
- Ruled from 1874-1914
- Thutob Namgyal, the ninth Chogyal of Sikkim (1874–1914), ruled during a period of British intervention, territorial disputes, and power struggles with Tibet. His reign saw the British-Sikkim War (1888), the appointment of J.C. White as the first Political Officer in Sikkim (1889), the 1890 Convention between Britain and China, and the shift of Sikkim's capital to Gangtok.

Shift of Capital from Tumlong to Gangtok
- Tumlong was no longer strategically viable, and Gangtok was better suited for trade and governance.
- In 1894, he moved the capital to Gangtok, which remains the capital of Sikkim today.
- Gangtok's development began with British support, including administrative offices and modern roads.

British Influence & Loss of Sikkim's Autonomy
- Initially, he tried to maintain strong ties with Tibet, but the British saw this as a threat.
- The British gradually increased their control over Sikkim, reducing his authority.

British-Sikkim War (1888) – Defeat of Tibetan Forces
- Tibet sent forces into Sikkim to challenge British influence, leading to war.
- The British decisively defeated the Tibetans in 1888 and expelled them from Sikkim.
- This war weakened Thutob Namgyal's authority and solidified British dominance.

J.C. White Appointed as First British Political Officer (1889)
- After the war, the British removed Thutob Namgyal from power and placed him under house arrest in Darjeeling.
- J.C. White was appointed as Sikkim's first British Political Officer (1889).

- The Chogyal lost direct control over administration, and British policies were imposed.

1890 Convention of Calcutta Between Britain & China

- In 1890, Britain and China signed a Convention without consulting the Chogyal.
- This agreement:
    - o   Recognized Sikkim as a British protectorate.
    - o   Defined the Sikkim-Tibet boundary along the Himalayas.
    - o   Allowed British trade with Tibet.
- Tibet refused to accept the agreement, leading to future conflicts.

1904 British Expedition to Tibet

- In 1904, Colonel Francis Younghusband led a British expedition to Tibet, forcing Tibet to open up to British trade.
- Thutob Namgyal, who had been restored to limited power by this time, was forced to cooperate with the British.

Development Under British Rule

- Despite losing political control, he helped develop Sikkim's infrastructure, roads, and modern administration under British supervision.
- Introduced legal and educational reforms with British support.
- Established Gangtok as the new administrative center.

Death & Establishment of STNM Hospital (1914)

- Died in 1914, after ruling for 40 years.
- Old STNM (Sir Thutob Namgyal Memorial) Hospital was built in his honor.
- Succeeded by Sidkeong Tulku Namgyal (his son), but he ruled for only a few months.

10. <u>Sidkeong Tulku Namgyal</u>

- Born 1879-Died 1914
- Ruled from 11 February 1914 - 5 December 1914, 10 Months
- Sidkeong Tulku Namgyal was the tenth Chogyal of Sikkim but ruled for only a **few months in 1914 (shortest ruling Chogyal of Sikkim)** before his sudden and mysterious death. He was a reformist ruler, attempting to modernize Sikkim's administration and reduce monastic control. His close ties with the British and his sudden death led to speculation and political intrigue.

Early Life & British Education

- Born in 1879, he was the son of Thutob Namgyal (9th Chogyal).
- Recognized as a Tibetan Buddhist reincarnate (Tulku) and educated in British India.
- Studied at St. Paul's School in Darjeeling and was trained under British officials to prepare for his future rule.

- Served as the de facto ruler of Sikkim in 1908 when his father became ill.

Close Relations with the British

- Had strong support from the British, especially the Political Officer J.C. White.
- The British favored him over Tibetan-backed factions in Sikkim's government.
- Promoted Western-style administration, road-building, and economic reforms.

Accession to the Throne (December 1913)

- Officially became the 10th Chogyal of Sikkim in December 1913 after the death of his father, Thutob Namgyal.
- Began introducing administrative and monastic reforms to modernize Sikkim.

Attempted Reforms & Opposition from Monasteries

- Sought to reduce the political power of Buddhist monasteries over the state.
- Planned land and taxation reforms to limit the control of powerful monastic estates.
- Faced strong resistance from the Buddhist clergy and Tibetan-backed factions.

Sudden & Mysterious Death (December 5, 1914)

- Died under mysterious circumstances within a few months of his rule.
- Officially reported as a heart attack, but rumors of poisoning spread, as his reforms angered powerful religious elites.
- His sudden death ended his modernization efforts, and the pro-Tibetan faction regained influence.

Succession & End of Reforms

- Succeeded by his half-brother Tashi Namgyal (11th Chogyal of Sikkim).

11. <u>Tashi Namgyal</u>

- Born 1893- Died 1963
- Ruled from 1914-1963, 49 years
- Tashi Namgyal, the eleventh Chogyal of Sikkim (1914–1963), is remembered as a progressive and reformist ruler. His reign saw major legal and economic reforms, closer ties with India, and efforts to maintain Sikkim's sovereignty during British rule and India's independence. He also introduced modern infrastructure, land reforms, and an independent judiciary.

Administrative & Judicial Reforms

- Established an independent judiciary in 1916.
- Abolished landlords' judicial and magistrate functions.
- Introduced modern judicial procedures based on Indian civil and criminal laws.

- Set up the **Sikkim High Court in April 1955**.

Political & Diplomatic Achievements

- Favoured closer ties between Sikkim, India, and Tibet.
- After India's independence in 1947, secured a special protectorate status for Sikkim.
- **1950 Indo-Sikkim Treaty** made Sikkim an Indian protectorate, with India managing its external affairs, defense, and strategic communications.
- Faced protests from political groups like the Sikkim State Congress, who demanded democracy and full accession to India.

Economic & Infrastructure Development

- Launched the Seven-Year Development Plan (1954–61) to modernize Sikkim's infrastructure.
- Established **Sikkim Nationalized Transport (SNT) in 1944** to improve connectivity.

Educational Reforms

- Founded **Tashi Namgyal Academy (TNA) in 1926**, which remains one of the premier schools in Sikkim today.

12. <u>Palden Thondup Namgyal</u>

- Born 1923-Died 1982
- Ruled from 1963-1975
- Palden Thondup Namgyal, the twelfth and last Chogyal of Sikkim (1963–1975), ruled during a period of political turmoil, democratic movements, and Sikkim's eventual merger with India. His reign saw rising internal dissent, growing Indian influence, and the abolition of the monarchy in 1975, leading to Sikkim's full integration into India.

Accession to the Throne (1963)

- Succeeded his father, Tashi Namgyal, as Chogyal of Sikkim in 1963.
- Unlike his father, who balanced relations with India, he sought greater independence for Sikkim, which led to tensions with the Indian government.

Establishment of Namgyal Institute of Tibetology (1958)

- Established **Namgyal Institute of Tibetology** in 1958, named after the 11th Chogyal of Sikkim, Sir Tashi Namgyal.
- The Institute's foundation stone was laid by the 14th Dalai Lama on 10th February, 1957, and the
- Institute was declared open by the late Prime Minister of India Pandit Jawaharlal Nehru on 1st October, 1958.
- The institute became a major center for the study of Tibetan Buddhism, history, language, and culture.
- NIT remains one of the world's most important centers for Tibetan studies today.

Rise of Pro-Democracy Movements & the Tripartite Agreement (1973)
- Faced increasing opposition from pro-democracy political parties like the Sikkim National Congress, which demanded an end to the monarchy and full democracy.
- Widespread protests erupted in 1973, with demands for electoral reforms and a more representative government.
- The crisis led to the signing of the Tripartite Agreement **(8 May 1973)** between:
    1. The Chogyal (Monarchy)
    2. The Government of India
    3. The Leaders of the Pro-Democracy Movement
- **Key Provisions of the Tripartite Agreement:**
    o Mandated democratic reforms in Sikkim, including the establishment of a legislative assembly and the conduct of elections.
    o The Sikkimese people were given greater political rights.

1974 Sikkim Government Act – Limited Monarchy
- After the May 8 agreement was signed, the Government of Sikkim Act, 1974, paved the way for setting up the first-ever democratically elected government in Sikkim and sought the state's representation in the political institutions of India.
- In the same year, Sikkim became an associate State of India.
- The Sikkim Assembly passed a law in 1974, reducing the Chogyal's powers and establishing a democratically elected government under Prime Minister Lhendup Dorji Kazi.
- India recognized Sikkim as an "Associate State" instead of a fully independent protectorate.
- The Chogyal opposed these changes, seeing them as a step towards India's complete control over Sikkim.

Merger with India (1975) – End of the Monarchy
- In April 1975, the Sikkimese Assembly passed a resolution abolishing the monarchy, citing the Chogyal's loss of public support.
- A referendum was held, where over 97% of Sikkimese people voted to join India.
- On May 16, 1975, Sikkim officially became the 22nd state of India, ending the rule of the Chogyal dynasty.

Later Life & Death (1982)
- After being deposed, Palden Thondup Namgyal lived in seclusion, mostly in India.
- He was diagnosed with cancer and later moved to New York for treatment.
- Passed away in 1982 in New York City, marking the end of the Namgyal dynasty's political role in Sikkim.

Towards Democracy

- The election was held in April 1974 in which Sikkim Congress headed by Kazi Lhendup Dorjee swept the polls by winning 31 of the 32 seats
- L.D. Kazi became the first CM.
- The Assembly that met on 10th April 1975 passed two important resolutions;
- First, the resolution demanding the abolition of the institution of Chogyal and second, the resolution of merger of Sikkim with India.
- Both the above-mentioned resolutions were passed unanimously by the House which was later endorsed by majority of people in a state-wide referendum held on the 14th April 1975.
- Sikkim became the 22nd Indian State on 26 April 1975. On **16 May 1975**, Sikkim officially became a state of the Indian Union.
- B.B. Lal was appointed the first Governor of Sikkim.

<u>35th Constitutional Amendment Act, 1974</u>

- **Purpose**: To make **Sikkim an "Associate State"** of India.
- **Background**:
  - Sikkim was a **protectorate** of India under the **Indo-Sikkim Treaty of 1950**.
  - Political instability and growing demand for democracy led to closer integration with India.
  - The Chogyal (king) of Sikkim was facing opposition from pro-democracy leaders.
  - The Sikkim Assembly passed a **resolution in 1974** seeking greater integration with India.
- **Key Provisions**:
  - Inserted **Article 2A** in the Constitution, recognizing Sikkim as an **Associate State**.
  - Added the **Tenth Schedule**, detailing Sikkim's special relationship with India.
  - Allowed the Sikkimese people to elect one representative to the **Lok Sabha** and the **Rajya Sabha**.
  - The Government of India gained more control over Sikkim's administration.
- **Impact**:
  - This amendment was an intermediate step before Sikkim became a full-fledged state.
  - It was short-lived, as political unrest continued, leading to the 36th Amendment.

<u>**36th Constitutional Amendment Act, 1975**</u>
- **Purpose**: To make **Sikkim the 22nd state of India**.
- **Background**:
  - Anti-monarchy protests intensified, and there was a demand for complete merger with India.
  - In April 1975, a referendum was held, where over 97% of Sikkimese people voted to join India.
  - The Indian Parliament moved quickly to formalize Sikkim's status.
- **Key Provisions**:
  - **Repealed Article 2A** (which had made Sikkim an Associate State).
  - Inserted **Article 371F**, providing **special provisions** for Sikkim (e.g., maintaining Sikkim's distinct identity and laws).
  - Sikkim became a **full-fledged state** under **Article 1** of the Indian Constitution.
  - The **Tenth Schedule (related to Associate State status) was removed**.
- **Impact**:
  - The Act was passed on April 26,1975 and Sikkim officially became the **22nd state of India** on **May 16, 1975**.
  - The Chogyal monarchy was abolished.
  - Sikkim's distinct cultural and legal identity was safeguarded through **Article 371F**.

<u>**Article 371F**</u>
- Article 371F, under **part XXI of the Indian Constitution** was included in the Constitution through the 36th Amendment to ensure that Sikkim's distinct identity and cultural heritage were protected and preserved after its merger with India.

1. Legislative Assembly
- Sikkim's Legislative Assembly was allowed to have only 30 members—a unique exception compared to other states.
- The **1974 elected Assembly** was recognized as the first Assembly under the Indian Constitution.
- Reserved seats for different communities to protect their interests.

2. Land Ownership and Property Rights
- Non-Sikkimese individuals are restricted from owning land in the state, a measure designed to protect the indigenous population's rights.
- Only the descendants of Sikkim subjects (those who lived in the state before its merger with India) whose names were mentioned in the **1961 register under the Sikkim Subject Regulation Act, 1961** are considered Sikkimese and are entitled to certain benefits, such as the right to own land and get state government jobs. They are also exempted from paying income tax.

3. Autonomy and Integration
- The Governor of Sikkim was given special discretion in ensuring the law and governance transition after Sikkim's integration into India.

4. Recognition of Sikkimese Laws
- Article 371F ensures that the judicial and administrative decisions made by Sikkim's authorities prior to its merger remain valid. It protects the continuity of their pre-merger legal system as an integral part of their governance.

Sikkim Subject Regulation Act, 1961

The Sikkim Subjects Regulation of 1961 was established to define the status of "Sikkim Subjects" and outline the criteria for acquiring or losing this status.

Key Provisions:
1. **Definition of Sikkim Subjects:**
   - Individuals domiciled in Sikkim before the regulation's commencement who:
     - Were born in Sikkim and reside there, or
     - Have resided in Sikkim for at least 15 years prior to the regulation.
   - Wives and minor children of such individuals are also considered Sikkim Subjects.
2. **Domicile Criteria:**
   - A person is considered domiciled in Sikkim if they have made it their permanent home and severed ties with their country of origin, such as by disposing of property there or acquiring property in Sikkim.
3. **Registration of Non-Domiciled Individuals:**
   - Persons not domiciled in Sikkim but whose ancestors were deemed Sikkim Subjects before 1850 can apply for registration as Sikkim Subjects, provided they haven't voluntarily acquired citizenship of another country.
4. **Descent:**
   - Individuals born after the regulation's commencement are Sikkim Subjects if their father was a Sikkim Subject at the time of their birth, regardless of the birthplace.
5. **Marriage:**
   - Foreign women marrying Sikkim Subjects after the regulation's commencement are generally eligible to register as Sikkim Subjects upon application.

This regulation played a crucial role in determining the legal status of individuals in Sikkim prior to its merger with India in 1975. Post-merger, the 36th Amendment to the Indian Constitution incorporated Sikkim as a state, and Article 371F was introduced to protect the rights and privileges of Sikkimese people, including those recognized under the 1961 regulation.

<u>**Income Tax Exemption for Sikkimese People**</u>
This exemption is provided under **Section 10(26AAA) of the Income Tax Act, 1961**, in line with Article 371F.
Key aspects of this provision are:
Income Exemptions:
- Income accruing or arising to a Sikkimese individual from any source in the State of Sikkim.
- Income by way of dividend or interest on securities.

Exceptions:
- The exemption does not apply to a Sikkimese woman who marries a non-Sikkimese individual on or after April 1, 2008.

Definition of "Sikkimese":
An individual qualifies as a "Sikkimese" if:
1. Their name was recorded in the register maintained under the Sikkim Subjects Regulation, 1961, immediately before April 26, 1975.
2. Their name was included in the Register of Sikkim Subjects by virtue of specific Government of India orders dated August 7, 1990, and April 8, 1991.
3. Their father's, husband's, paternal grandfather's, or brother's name from the same father appears in the Register of Sikkim Subjects, even if their own name does not.

Recent Supreme Court verdict

In a landmark decision on **January 13, 2023**, the Supreme Court of India expanded the scope of income tax exemptions under Section 10(26AAA) of the Income Tax Act, 1961, for individuals in Sikkim. The court addressed two primary issues:

1. **Inclusion of Old Indian Settlers:**
    - Previously, the definition of "Sikkimese" under Section 10(26AAA) excluded Indian citizens who had settled in Sikkim before its merger with India on April 26, 1975, unless their names were recorded in the Sikkim Subjects Register. The Supreme Court found this exclusion discriminatory and unconstitutional, ruling that all Indian settlers residing in Sikkim before the merger are entitled to income tax exemptions, irrespective of their inclusion in the Sikkim Subjects Register.

2. **Rights of Sikkimese Women:**
    - The proviso to Section 10(26AAA) denied tax exemptions to Sikkimese women who married non-Sikkimese individuals after April 1, 2008. The court deemed this proviso arbitrary and discriminatory, violating Articles 14 (Right to Equality), 15 (Prohibition of Discrimination), and 21 (Right to Life and Personal Liberty) of the Indian Constitution. Consequently, this proviso was struck down, ensuring that Sikkimese women retain their tax exemptions regardless of their spouse's origin

Sikkim State Leadership (As of Feb 2025)

- Chief Minister - **P.S Golay**
- Governor – **Om Prakash Mathur**
- Chief Justice of Sikkim High Court - **Biswanath Somadder**
- DGP – **Akshay Sachdeva**
- Chief Secretary – **R. Telang**
- Speaker of SLA – **Mingma Norbu Sherpa**
- Deputy Speaker of SLA – **Raj Kumari Thapa**
- Gangtok Mayor - **Nell Bahadur Chettri**

Sikkim Legislative Assembly Cabinet

1. **Shri Prem Singh Tamang** – Hon'ble Chief Minister
   - Excise Department
   - Finance Department
   - Home Department
   - Information & Public Relations Department
   - Information Technology Department
   - Land Revenue & Disaster Management Department
   - Planning & Development Department
   - Power Department
   - Skill Development Department
   - Transport Department
2. **Shri Puran Kumar Gurung** –
   - Agriculture Department
   - Animal Husbandry & Veterinary Services Department
   - Fisheries Department
   - Horticulture Department
3. **Shri Tshering Thendup Bhutia** –
   - Commerce & Industries Department
   - Tourism & Civil Aviation Department
4. **Shri Bhim Hang Limboo** –
   - Buildings & Housing Department
   - Labour Department
5. **Shri Pintso Namgyal Lepcha** –
   - Forest & Environment Department
   - Mines & Geology Department
   - Science & Technology Department
6. **Shri Raju Basnet** –
   - Education Department

- o   Law Department
    - o   Sports & Youth Affairs Department
7. **Shri N.B. Dahal** –
    - o   Roads & Bridges Department
8. **Shri G.T. Dhungel** –
    - o   Culture Department
    - o   Health & Family Welfare Department
9. **Shri Bhoj Raj Rai** –
    - o   Food & Civil Supplies Department
    - o   Urban Development Department
10. **Shri Sonam Lama** –
    - o   Ecclesiastical Department
    - o   Public Health Engineering Department
    - o   Water Resources Department
11. **Shri Samdup Lepcha** –
    - o   Printing & Stationery Department
    - o   Social Welfare Department
    - o   Women & Child Development Department
12. **Shri Arun Upreti** –
    - o   Cooperation Department
    - o   Rural Development Department

First in Sikkim

Chief Ministers of Sikkim

1. Kazi Lhendup Dorjee (16 May 1975 - 18 August 1979)
2. N.B. Bhandari (18 October 1979 - 11 May 1984) (again from 8 March 1985 - 17 June 1994)
3. B.B. Gurung (11 May 1984 - 25 May 1984) (Shortest ruling C.M - 13 days)
4. Sanchaman Limboo (17 June 1994 - 12 December 1994)
5. Pawan Kumar Chamling (12 December 1994 - 27 May 2019)
6. Prem Singh Tamang (27 May 2019 - *Incumbent*)

The **first Speaker** of the Sikkim Legislative Assembly was Shri C.S. Roy.

Governors of Sikkim

	Name	Took office	Left office
1	B. B. Lal	18 May 1975	9 January 1981
2	Homi J. H. Taleyarkhan	10 January 1981	17 June 1984
3	Kona Prabhakar Rao	18 June 1984	30 May 1985
—	Bhishma Narain Singh *(additional charge)*	31 May 1985	20 November 1985
4	T.V. Rajeswar	21 November 1985	1 March 1989
5	S.K. Bhatnagar	2 March 1989	7 February 1990
6	Radhakrishna Hariram Tahiliani	8 February 1990	20 September 1994
7	P. Shiv Shankar	21 September 1994	11 November 1995
—	K.V. Raghunatha Reddy *(additional charge)*	12 November 1995	9 February 1996
8	Chaudhary Randhir Singh	10 February 1996	17 May 2001

9	Kidar Nath Sahani	18 May 2001	25 October 2002
10	V. Rama Rao	26 October 2002	12 July 2006
—	R.S. Gavai *(acting)*	13 July 2006	12 August 2006
(10)	V. Rama Rao	13 August 2006	25 October 2007
11	Sudarshan Agarwal	25 October 2007	8 July 2008
12	Balmiki Prasad Singh	9 July 2008	30 June 2013
13	Shriniwas Dadasaheb Patil[1]	1 July 2013	26 August 2018
14	Ganga Prasad	26 August 2018[2]	12 February 2023
15	Lakshman Acharya	13 February 2023	30 July 2024
16	Om Prakash Mathur	31 July 2024	*Incumbent*

First in Sikkim

- First Woman legislative member - **Kumari Hemlata Chettri**
- First Woman speaker of SLA - **Kalawati Subba**
- First Woman Minister - **R. Ongmoo**
- First DGP - **TN Tenzing**
- First Deputy CM - **PT Lucksom**
- First Speaker SLA- **Chatur Singh Roy**
- First Chief Engineer - **Fakir Chand Jali**
- First Election Commissioner - **RN Sengupta**
- First Woman Judge - **Menakshi Madan Rasaily**
- First Chogyal - **Phuntsok Namgyal**
- Last Chogyal - **Palden Thondup Namgyal**
- First Capital - **Yuksom**
- First Governor - **B.B Lal**
- First Chief Justice of Sikkim High Court - **Man Mohan Singh Gujral**
- First person from Sikkim to climb Mount Everest - **Sonam Gyatso (1965)**

Jaslal Pradhan
- Sikkim's first Olympian Arjuna Awardee
- He competed in 1984 Summer Olympics (Los Angeles)

Festivals of Sikkim

1. Maghe Sankranti
- First day of the tenth month of the Bikram Sambat calendar which heralds the onset of warmer weather is a major secular festival of the Nepalese.
- Falls on the 14 January every year
- Bathing festival called Makkar is observed, when people take a dip at the confluence of the Tista and Rangit.

2. Losar
- Tibetan New Year which falls in the month of February
- Two days prior to Losar, the Gutor Chaam is performed at Rumtek monastery depicting the battle between good and evil and the ritualized destruction of evil.

3. Sonam Lochar
- Important festival of Tamang community
- Festival falls in the month January / February (Magha Sukla Pakcha) Spring season.

4. Ramnawami (Chaite Dasain)
- The festival, also known as 'Small Dashain' is commonly celebrated as 'Ram Navami' in other parts of the country, commemorating the birth of Lord Rama.
- Typically occurs in the months of March or April every year.

5. Saga Dawa
- Saga Dawa or the Triple Blessed Festival is an auspicious month for the Sikkimese Buddhists with prayers held throughout the month in various monasteries.
- On the full moon of this 4th month of the Tibetan calendar (April / May month) [celebrated as Buddha Purnima in the rest of India] is the main celebration.
- Believed that on this day the Buddha was born, attained Enlightenment and achieved nirvana.

6. Bhanu Jayanti
- 13 July
- Birthday of Bhanubhakta Acharya, who is also more popularly known as "Nepal ka Adikavi" (Nepal's first poet).
- First Nepali poet who translated the great epic "Ramayana" from Sanskrit to Nepali.

7. **Drukpa Tshechi**
   - Celebrated on the 4th day (Tsheshi) of the 6th month (Drukpa) of the Tibetan Calendar.
   - Falls somewhere around July or August each year.
   - Observed to celebrate Lord Buddha and his first preaching of the Four Noble Truths.

8. **Tendong Lho Rum Faat**
   - One of the oldest festivals of the Lepchas and is usually held in August.
   - The 3-day celebrations begin with the offering of prayers to Mount Tendong in South Sikkim.
   - Legend has it that Mt. Tendong saved the Lepcha people during the great deluge which flooded the entire Mayel Lyang country, now known as Sikkim. The festival is an annual thanksgiving to the saviour mountain.
   - Various literary and cultural programmes are held in the state capital to commemorate the occasion. On the concluding day, exhibits on traditional Lepcha food, costumes and ornaments are displayed.

9. **Guru Rimpoche's Thunkar Tshechu**
   - Birth anniversary of Guru Padmasambhava, the founder of Tibetan Buddhism who first introduced Buddhism in Sikkim and other neighbouring Himalayan regions during 8th century.
   - It falls on the tenth day of the fifth Tibetan month (July/ August)
   - Chaams are held at Rumtek monastery celebrating different episodes from his life.

10. **Indra Jatra**
   - August/ September
   - Indra Jatra or "Yenya" is the biggest festival for the Nepalese "NEWAR" community in Sikkim
   - Named after the Hindu God of Rain and also the King of Heaven, Lord Indra, the festival's prime objective is to seek his blessings in the form of rains and showers.
   - The legend of the festival goes back to the Vedic times when Lord Indra was imprisoned by the people of Kathmandu Valley, after having him caught stealing the rare and fragrant 'Parijat Flowers' from the valley for his mother. It is then when the people realized who he actually was, they released him and promised to dedicate one of the most colourful festivals to him, also in return requesting him to visit the valley every year, thereby blessing it with rains and prosperity.

11. **Pang-Lhabsol**
   - Commemorates the consecration of Mount Khangchendzonga as the guardian deity of Sikkim.
   - It is believed that the mountain god played an active role in introducing Buddhism into this former kingdom. According to a handwritten biography by Lhatsun Chenpo, the chief propagator of Buddhism in Sikkim, it was divine visions sent by the mountain god which guided him to Demajong (the hidden valley of rice, as Sikkim is referred to by the Bhutias).
   - To this day the mountain god is invoked and prayed upon at Pang Lhabsol to continue protecting Sikkim.
   - The festival is celebrated on the 15th day of the 7th month of the Tibetan calendar corresponding to late August/early September.
   - The festival also marks the commemoration of blood brotherhood sworn between the Lepchas and the Bhutias at Kabi in the 15th century.

12. **Durga Puja (Dassain)**
   - Takes place in the month of September/ October
   - The puja of Goddess Durga is performed from the first day (Prathama) to the ninth day (Navmi).
   - On the tenth day, the elders in every family apply 'tika' on the young ones and bless them.

13. **Deepawali (Laxmi Puja)**
   - According to the legend, Lord Ram's return to Ayodhya after fourteen years in exile was celebrated on this particular day by lighting of earthen lamps all over.

14. **Lhabab Duechen**
   - Generally, in November
   - On the sacred day of Lhabab Duchen, followers of Buddhism throng to monasteries to light butter lamps, burn incense and offer special prayers to Lord Buddha; monks and lamas spend whole day reading the holy scriptures and purifying the air with their chanting of mantras.
   - This holy festival is marked by placing freshly painted ladders on the rocks by the monasteries to symbolize holy descent of Buddha from Trayastrimsa (The Heaven of Thirty-Three).

15. **Teyongsi Srijunga Sawan Tongnam**
   - Observed by the Limboo Community in Sikkim, Teyongsi Sirijunga Sawan Tongnam, marks the birth anniversary of the famous 18th

century scholar Teyongsi Sirijunga, who is greatly remembered for his legendary role as a revivalist of the Limboo's age old traditional legacy in the state.

16. Barahimizong

- December/ January
- Festival observed by the Mangar Community in Sikkim.
- Celebrated as a day when Mangar people come together to pay homage to their forefathers and kuldevtaas by performing various religious rituals and rites.
- The first Barahimizong Festival was held in 1998 with the prime objective of keeping alive, the cultural and traditional heritage of the community. It was with the efforts of the "Akhil Sikkim Mangar Sangh (ASMS)" and the "State Government of Sikkim" that the festival was a great success at its first event itself.

17. Sakewa

- Usually in December
- One of the most significant cultural and religious festivals for the Kirat Khambu Rai community in Sikkim.
- Celebrated as a homage to Mother Earth, it commences by performing Bhumi Puja followed by community dances and other rituals.
- The Kirat Rai people are believed to be some of the most ancient people of Himalayas. They are said to be nature worshippers and this tradition of theirs offering reverence to nature gods, praying for the well-being of all living creatures around the world, has been existing since ancient times.

18. Kagyed Dance

- December / January
- One of the most popular Buddhist festivals, Kagyed Chaam, is a celebration that is marked by masked monks and lamas performing some rigorous dance moves, symbolizing destruction of all the evil and negative forces, thereby bringing in peace and prosperity for one and all in the upcoming new year.

19. Losoong/Namsoong

- Mostly celebrated in the month of December
- Losoong also called Namsoong by the Lepchas is usually the time when the farmers rejoice and celebrate their harvest.
- The Black Hat dance takes place at this festival commemorating the victory of good over evil, with 'chaams' held in many monasteries two days prior to Losoong.
- Celebrated both by Bhutias & Lepchas

20. **Tamu Lochar**
   - Traditional festival of the Gurung Community
   - It marks the beginning of the Gurung New Year which falls on the 15th day of Pusa, according Vikram Sambat and 30th December in English Calendar.

Music & Dance of Sikkim

- Nepali folk dance "**Maruni**" – It is one of the oldest and popular group dance form of the **Nepali community**, usually performed by three male dancers and the three female dancers. The dancers are usually accompanied by a clown called "**Dhatu waray**". Sometimes Maruni dances are performed to the accompaniment of the **nine-instrument orchestra** known as "**Nau-mati Baja**"
- Nepali folk dance "**Tamamg Selo**"-This group dance of **Tamang community** is performed to the rhythmic sound of "**Dhamphu**", a musical instrument and hence are also called "Dhamphu" dance.
- **Bhutia** folk dance "**Tashi Sabdo**"-This age-old group dance beautifully and gracefully shows the customs of offering khadas (Scarfs) On auspicious occasion. The dancers dance to the melodious tunes dully supported by musical instrument such as Yarkha, Drum, Flute and Yangjey.

Lepcha Folk Dances

1. Chu-Faat
- Literal meaning of Chu is Snowy Range, while that of Faat is Worship. This group folk dance is performed in the honour of Mount Khangchendzonga, the guardian deity of the Sikkimese people.

2. Tendong Lho Rum Faat
- It is based on a famous Lepcha folk lore often retold to the new generation of Lepchas in the form of lyrical poetry. According to the legend, this group dance is performed to save people from the onslaught of mighty, mountainous rivers, First, the Lepchas living on the Tendong Hill in South Sikkim are reported to have offered prayers to the God through this dance

3. Zo-Mal-Lok
- This famous folk dance of Lepcha community shows normal activities such as sowing, reaping and harvesting of paddy.

<u>**Nepali Folk Dances**</u>

1. Chutkay
- Through this romantic group dance, performed by a group of male and female dancers, joys of life and feeling of happiness is shared during the harvesting season and on some other happy occasions.

2. Chyap-Brung
- Chyap-Brung is the traditional musical instrument of the **Limboo** community. It is like a Dholak in shape but much bigger in size. During the course of group dance, male dancers hang the instrument around their necks with the help of a rope and beat the drum with an open palm on one side and a stick on the other.

3. Naumati
- In this beautiful group dance of Damai community nine kinds of musical instruments are used to perfection. These are two types of Senai (Shehnai), Turhi, small and big, Damaha (Nagara) of two types, Tuyamko (Small Dhol) of two types, Dholki and Jhyamta (cymbal). The Naumati Baja is a regular feature during the wedding and other auspicious occasions.

4. Tamang Selo
- This group dance of **Tamang** community with robust foot tapping and elaborate sound and display of Damphu instrument is performed on all happy occasions. It highlights vigour and vitality of the community. Tamang songs known as ' **Hwai**' are full of human emotions.

<u>**Bhutia Folk Dances**</u>

1. Denong-Neh-Nah
- This group dance comprising of boys and girls is performed to pay homage to the past saints such as Guru Rimpoche and present saints in order to get their blessings.

2. Kagyed Dance
- Kagyed actually means the oral transmission of the eight Tantric Gods found in Tantric Buddhism. Kagyed Chham is a word of Bhutia origin. *'Ka'* means 'oral transmission', *'Gyed'* means 'eight' and *'Chham'* means ritualistic dance. This ritualistic dance is held every year in various Sikkimese Monastery. It is a time of celebration for the Bhutias as they welcome the New Year.

3. **Ta-Shi-Yang-Ku**
- A group of boys and girls through this dance try to invoke benign deities to shower fortunes on their home. They remember some animal deities also to bring good fortune and prosperity to the people. It is also performed during the consecration of a new house and to bless a newly married couple.

4. **Yak Chham**
- This dance depicts the movements of the yak and the simple lifestyle of the herdsmen of the mountains. The dancers don the costume and mask of the yak, and tune their steps to traditional songs and instrumental music.

Sikkim Award Winners

- **Sikkim** was **declared** as the first **organic farming state** of India on **18 January 2016.**

Sonam Gyatso
- Padma Bhusan (1965), Padma Shri (1962), Arjuna Award (1965)
- He was the second Indian man, the seventeenth man in world and the first person from Sikkim to summit Mount Everest the highest peak in the world

Padma Shri Winners
- Sonam Gyatso - 1962 (Sports) (Mountaineer)
- Sonam Wangyal - 1965 (Sports) (Mountaineer). He is the third Indian man and eighteenth man in world that climbed Mount Everest.
- Phu Dorjee - 1984 (Sports) (Mountaineer)
- Danny Denzongpa - 2003 (Art)
- Gadul Singh Lama (Sanu Lama) - 2005 (Literature & Education). Also, winner of Sahitya Akademi Award (1993)
- Sonam Tshering lepcha - 2007 (Art) (Folk Musician)
- Bhaichung Bhutia - 2008 (Sports) (Football). Also, Arjuna Award (1998)
- Keepu Tsering Lepcha - 2009 (Social Work)
- Norden Tshering Bhutia - 2009 (Literature & Education)
- Kedar Gurung - 2012 (Literature and Education)
- Hilda Mit Lepcha - 2013 (Folk Music)
- Birkha Bdr Muringla - 2017 (Literature and Education)
- Droupadi Ghimirey - 2019 (Social Work)
- Tarundeep Rai - 2020 (Sports). Also, Arjuna Award (2005)
- Khandu Wangchuk Bhutia - 2022 (Art)
- Shri Tula Ram Upreti - 2023 (Agriculture)
- Shri Jordan Lepcha - 2024 (Art)
- Shri Naren Gurung – 2025 (Art)

Gallantry Award Winners
- Sanjog Chhetri - Ashoka Chakra (2004, posthumously). Youngest recipient of the Ashoka Chakra (died aged 20 in 2003)
- Sonam Tamang - Shaurya Chakra (2021)

Buddhism

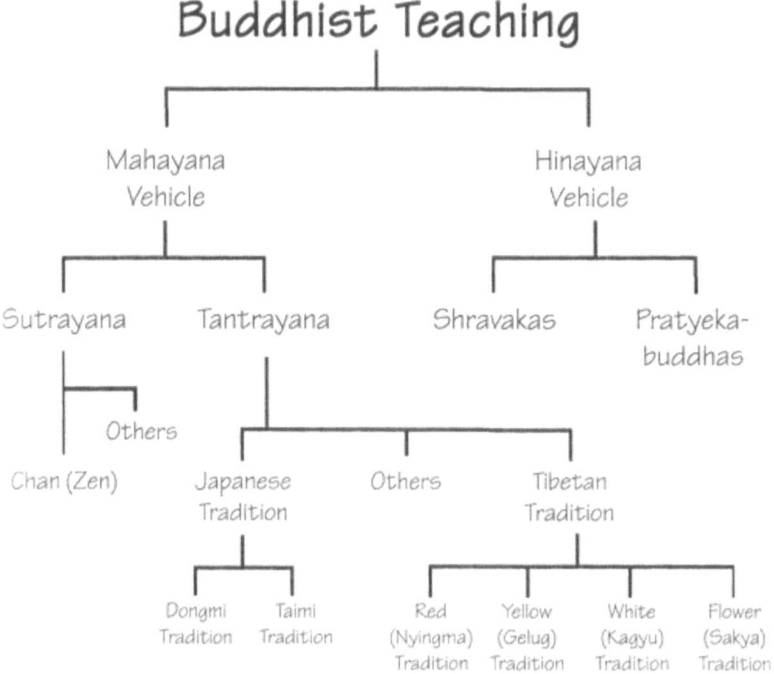

Schools of Tibetan Buddhism

1.) **Gelugpa (The Yellow hats)**
- Third **Dalai lama** took Mongol help to establish Gelugpa rule.
- **Grabbed power in 1642** under 5th dalai lama
- Emphasize study of logic and philosophy
- **Main leaders- <u>14th Dalai Lama and 11th Panchen Lama</u>**
- **Seat in Tibet - Potala**
- Current Location - Dharmashala (Dalai Lama)

2.) **Kagyupa (the Black hats)**
- Ruled Tibet before being dislodged by 5th Dalai Lama
- Called Black hats because of Karmapa's black crown
- **Main leaders - 17th Karmapa Lama**
- **Seats of Power - Tsurphu (Tibet) and Rumtek (Sikkim)**

- Current Location - Gyuto Tantric Monastery, Dharmashala

3.) Nyingma (The Red Hats)
- Oldest Buddhist Order **founded by Padmashambhava (Guru Rinpoche)** (8th century Buddhist Master), brahmin from present day Odisha, who took buddhism to tibet.
- Founded on translations of Buddhist scriptures from Sanskrit to Tibetian in 8th century.
- **Main Leader - Kathok getse Rinpoche** (born 1954), appointed in Bodh gaya in january 2018.

4.) Sakya (the Red hats)
- Similar to Nyimgma, head is **Sakya Pandita** who also wears a red hat.
- In 13th and 14th centuries, Sakyas dominated Tibet.
- Headship passes from uncle to nephew.

Summary
- Gelugpa - Yellow Hat (Dalai Lama)
- Kagyupa - Black Hat (Karmapa)
- Nyingma - Red Hat (Padmasambhava)
- Sakya - Red Hat

Noble Eightfold Path
- Right Understanding
- Right Thought
- Right Speech
- Right Action
- Right Livelihood
- Right Effort
- Right Mindfulness
- Right Concentration

Monastries in Sikkim

Dubdi Monastery
- Nyingma Sect
- Established in 1701, it is professed to be the <u>oldest monastery</u> in Sikkim and is located on the top of a hill which is about an hour's walk (3 kilometres (1.9 mi)) from Yuksom.

Rumtek Monastery
- Kargyu sect of Tibetan Buddhism
- Seat of His Holiness the Gyalwa Karmapa of the Kargyu sect of Buddhism
- Largest monastery in Sikkim

Enchey Monastery
- Nyingma of Vajrayana Buddhism
- 3 km to the northeast of Gangtok

Kartok Monastery
- Nyingma Sect
- Yuksom
- One of the popular sites to visit in Yuksom the Kartok forms a great combo with Dubdi and Ngadak Monastery.

Lingdum Monastery
- Also known as Ranka Monastery
- Kagyu Sect
- Recent monastery, completed in 1998

Pemayangtse Monastery
- Nyingma Sect
- Near Pelling
- Planned, designed and founded by Lama Lhatsun Chempo in 1647, it is one of the oldest and premier monasteries of Sikkim, also the most famous in Sikkim. Originally started as a small Lhakhang, it was subsequently enlarged during the reign of the third Chogyal Chakdor Namgyal and Khenchen Rolpai Dorjee in the year 1705 and consecrated by the third Lhatsun Chenpo Dzogchen Jigme Pawo in the year 1710 C.E.

Ralang Monastery
- Kagyu Sect
- Ravangla, South Sikkim

One Liners
- Dalai Lama is a title given by the Tibetan people to the foremost spiritual leader of the Gelug or "Yellow Hat" school of Tibetan Buddhism
- Buddhist master Padmasambhava., also known as "The Lotus-born," "Precious Guru" (Guru Rinpoche), or "The Second Buddha," Padmasambhava is widely credited with bringing Buddhism to the Tibetan lands.

- Tawang Monastery, located in Tawang city of Tawang district in Arunachal Pradesh, is the largest monastery in India and second largest in the world after the Potala Palace in Lhasa, Tibet. Tawang Monastery is known in Tibetan as Gaden Namgyal Lhatse, which translates to "the divine paradise of complete victory." It was founded by Merak Lama Lodre Gyatso in 1680-1681 in accordance with the wishes of the 5th Dalai Lama, Ngawang Lobsang Gyatso. It belongs to the Gelug school of Vajrayana Buddhism

Tabo Monastery
- Situated at the height of 10,007 feet in Lahaul and Spiti district of Himachal Pradesh
- Known as the 'Ajanta of the Himalayas'
- Established in 996 CE
- Gelug sect

North Eastern Council

- **North Eastern Council** (NEC) is a statutory advisory body constituted under the North Eastern Council Act 1971 and came into being on 7 **November 1972 at Shillong**
- The eight States of Northeast India viz.
- Arunachal Pradesh
- Assam
- Manipur
- Meghalaya
- Mizoram
- Nagaland
- Tripura
- Sikkim
- They are represented by their respective Chief Ministers and Governors.
- **Sikkim** was added to the council in the year **2002**. The **headquarters** of the council is situated in **Shillong** and functions under the Ministry of Development of North Eastern Region (DONER) of the Government of India.

UN & Other Important World Organizations

The United Nations

- The United Nations (UN) is an international organization established on 24 October 1945, which aims to maintain international peace and security.
- The UN was established after World War II with the aim of preventing future wars, succeeding the ineffective **League of Nations**
- Headquarters: **New York City**
- Its Official Languages are Arabic, Chinese, English, French, Russian and Spanish.
- Mnemonic - Official languages of UN: **FARCES** (French, Arabic, Russian, Chinese, English, Spanish)
- The United Nations has six principal organs:

1. The General Assembly,
2. the Security Council,
3. the Economic and Social Council,
4. the Trusteeship Council,
5. the International Court of Justice, and
6. the UN Secretariat.

All were established in 1945 when the UN was founded.

- Trusteeship Council suspended its operation on 1 November 1994, and although under the United Nations Charter it continues to exist on paper, its future role and even existence remains uncertain.

General Assembly
- The General Assembly is the main deliberative, policy making and representative organ of the UN
- It is the only body which includes representatives from all member countries. Each member country has one vote

Security Council
- The Security Council has primary responsibility for the maintenance of international peace and security
- The Security Council is composed of 15 Members: Five permanent members: China, France, Russia, the United Kingdom, and the United States, and ten non-permanent members elected for two-year terms by the General Assembly

- Mnemonic - Permanent members of UNSC: FARCE (France, America, Russia, China, England)

International Court of Justice
- The International Court of Justice is the principal judicial organ of the United Nations
- Headquarters: The Hague, Netherlands
- It is the only one of the six principal organs of the United Nations not located in New York
- The International Court of Justice is composed of 15 judges elected to nine-year terms of office by the United Nations General Assembly and the Security Council.

Economic and Social Council
- The Council has 54 Members, which are elected yearly by the General Assembly for overlapping three-year terms
- The Council is the principal body for coordination, policy review, policy dialogue and recommendations on economic, social and environmental issues, as well as implementation of internationally agreed development goals

Secretariat
- The Secretary-General is chief administrative officer of the Organization, appointed by the General Assembly on the recommendation of the Security Council for a five-year, renewable term

<u>Specialized organizations and agencies of the United Nations</u>

- UN specialized agencies are international organizations that coordinate their work with the United Nations through negotiated agreements.

Sl. No.	Organization Name	Headquarters	Founded
1.	Food and Agriculture Organization (FAO)	Rome, Italy	1945
2.	International Civil Aviation Organization (ICAO)	Montreal, Canada	1947
3.	International Fund for Agricultural Development (IFAD)	Rome, Italy	1977

4.	International Labour Organization (ILO)	Geneva, Switzerland	1919
5.	International Maritime Organization (IMO)	London, United Kingdom	1959
6.	International Monetary Fund (IMF)	Washington, D.C., United States	1947
7.	International Telecommunications Union (ITU)	Geneva, Switzerland	1865
8.	United Nations Educational, Scientific and Cultural Organization (UNESCO)	Paris, France	1946
9.	United Nations Industrial Development Organization (UNIDO)	Vienna, Austria	1966
10.	Universal Postal Union (UPU)	Bern, Switzerland	1875
11.	World Health Organization (WHO)	Geneva, Switzerland	1948
12.	World Intellectual Property Organization	Geneva, Switzerland	1967
13.	World Meteorological Organization (WMO)	Geneva, Switzerland	1950
14.	World Tourism Organization (UNWTO)	Madrid, Spain	1975
15.	World Bank Group: 1. IBRD: International Bank for Reconstruction and Development 2. IDA: International Development Association 3. IFC: International Finance Corporation	Washington, D.C., United States	 1945 1960 1956

Bretton Woods Conference

- The United Nations Monetary and Financial Conference (1944), commonly known as Bretton Wood conference, was held in Bretton Woods, New Hampshire, USA to regulate the international monetary and financial order after the conclusion of World War II.
- The conference resulted in the agreements to set up the International Bank for Reconstruction and Development (IBRD) popularly known as World Bank and the International Monetary Fund (IMF). The IMF was set up to foster monetary stability at global level.
- The IBRD was created to speed up post-war reconstruction. The two institutions are known as the Bretton Woods twins.

The European Union

- The European Union (EU) is an international organization made up of **27 European countries**
- The Union currently counts 27 EU countries. The United Kingdom withdrew from the European Union on 31 January 2020.
- Under **Article 50 of the Lisbon Treaty**, members can **withdraw** from the European Union.
- The capital of European union: **Brussels, Belgium**
- **Official motto** of the European Union: **United in diversity**
- **Member Countries**

1.	Austria	15.	Estonia
2.	Italy	16.	Portugal
3.	Belgium	17.	Finland
4.	Latvia	18.	Romania
5.	Bulgaria	19.	France
6.	Lithuania	20.	Slovakia
7.	Croatia	21.	Germany
8.	Luxembourg	22.	Slovenia
9.	Cyprus	23.	Greece
10.	Malta	24.	Spain
11.	Czech Republic	25.	Hungary
12.	Netherlands	26.	Sweden
13.	Denmark	27.	Ireland
14.	Poland		

- The euro (€) is the official currency of 19 out of 27 EU countries. These countries are collectively known as the Eurozone.
- **Eurozone Countries**: Austria, Belgium, Cyprus, Estonia, Finland, France, Germany, Greece, Ireland, Italy, Latvia, Lithuania, Luxembourg, Malta, the Netherlands, Portugal, Slovakia, Slovenia, Spain
- **Non-Eurozone Countries**: Bulgaria, Croatia, Czech Republic, Hungary, Poland, Romania, Sweden. These are countries where the euro has still not been adopted, but who will join once they have met the necessary conditions.

International Organizations

African union
- The African Union is a continental union consisting of 55 member states located on the continent of Africa.
- Headquarters: Addis Ababa, Ethiopia
- Founded: 9 July 2002, Durban, South Africa

The Arab league
- The Arab League, formally the League of Arab States, is a regional organization in the Arab world.
- Headquarters: Cairo, Egypt
- The 22 members of the Arab League are Algeria, Bahrain, Comoros, Djibouti, Egypt, Iraq, Jordan, Kuwait, Lebanon, Libya, Mauritania, Morocco, Oman, Palestine, Qatar, Saudi Arabia, Somalia, Sudan, Syria, Tunisia, the United Arab Emirates and Yemen

The Asia-Pacific Economic Cooperation (APEC)
- The Asia-Pacific economic cooperation was founded in 1989 to further cooperation on trade and investment between nations of the region.
- Headquarters: Singapore
- The 21 members of the Asia-Pacific economic cooperation are Australia, Brunei, Canada, Chile, China, Hong Kong, China, Indonesia, Japan, Malaysia, Mexico, New Zealand, Papua New Guinea, Peru, The Philippines, Russia, Singapore, Republic of Korea, Chinese Taipei, Thailand, and Vietnam.
- India is not a member of APEC. It is an observer country

Association of South-East Asian Nations (ASEAN)
- Headquarters: Jakarta, Indonesia
- Founded: 8 August 1967
- The members of the Association of South-East Asian Nations are Brunei, Myanmar, Cambodia, Indonesia, Laos, Malaysia, the Philippines, Singapore, Thailand and Vietnam.
- Mnemonic - MBBS CLIP TV (Malaysia, Burma, Brunei, Singapore, Cambodia, Laos, Indonesia, Phillipines, Thailand, Vietnam)
- Timor Leste is 11th Member added in Nov 2022

The Commonwealth
- Headquarters: London, United Kingdom
- The Commonwealth of Nations is a political association of 54 member states, mostly former territories of the British Empire

The Group of Seven (G7)
- Founded: 1975
- The Group of Seven (G7) Members: United States, Japan, Canada, Italy, United Kingdom, France, Germany
- Mnemonic to remember JUICE with GF - Japan, US, Italy, Canada, England (UK), Germany, France
- G8 Countries - With Russia

Group of Twenty (G20)
- Founded: 26 September 1999
- The G20 comprises 19 countries and the European Union. The 19 countries are Argentina, Australia, Brazil, Canada, China, Germany, France, India, Indonesia, Italy, Japan, Mexico, Russia, Saudi Arabia, South Africa, South Korea, Turkey, the United Kingdom and the United States.
- Mnemonic - GURU JI SITA AB SSC FCI ME job karti hai (Germany, USA, Russia, United Kingdom, Japan, India, Saudi Arabia, Indonesia, Turkey, Australia, Argentina, Brazil, South Africa, South Korea, Canada, France, China, Italy, Mexico, European Union)

The North Atlantic Treaty Organization (NATO)
- Headquarters: Brussels, Belgium
- Founded: 1949
- The 29 member states of NATO are Albania, Belgium, Bulgaria, Canada, Croatia, Czech Republic, Denmark, Estonia, France, Germany, Greece, Hungary, Iceland, Italy, Latvia, Lithuania, Luxembourg, Montenegro, Netherlands, Norway, Poland, Portugal, Romania, Slovakia, Slovenia, Spain, Turkey, United Kingdom and United States.

The Organization of the Petroleum Exporting Countries (OPEC)
- Headquarters: Vienna, Austria
- Founded: 1960
- The current OPEC members are Algeria, Angola, Congo, Ecuador, Equatorial Guinea, Gabon, Iran, Iraq, Kuwait, Libya, Nigeria, Saudi Arabia, United Arab Emirates and Venezuela
- Mnemonic - KILVIS AUR ANGE (Kuwait, Iran, Libya, Venezuela, Iraq, Saudi Arabia, Algeria, UAE, Republic of Congo, Angola, Nigeria, Gabon, Equatorial Guinea)

The South Asian Association for Regional Cooperation (SAARC)
- Founded: 1985
- Headquarters of SAARC: Kathmandu, Nepal

- The member states are Afghanistan, Bangladesh, Bhutan, India, the Maldives, Nepal, Pakistan and Sri Lanka
- Mnemonic - MBBS PAIN (Maldives, Bangladesh, Bhutan, Sri Lanka, Pakistan, Afghanistan, India, Nepal)

BIMSTEC
- The BIMSTEC member states are Bangladesh, India, Myanmar, Sri Lanka, Thailand, Nepal
- Headquarters: Dhaka, Bangladesh
- Founded:1997
- Mnemonic - MBBS NIT (Myanmar, Bangladesh, Bhutan, Sri Lanka, Nepal, India, Thailand)

The World Trade Organization (WTO)
- Headquarters: Geneva, Switzerland.
- The WTO has 164 members and 23 observer governments

Shanghai cooperation organisation (SCO)
- Headquarters: Beijing, China
- Formation: 2001
- The SCO comprises eight Member States: China, India, Kazakhstan, Kyrgyzstan, Russia, Pakistan, Tajikistan and Uzbekistan

International Solar Alliance (ISA)
- Headquarters: Gurugram, India
- Founded: 30 November 2015
- The International Solar Alliance (ISA) is an alliance of 121 countries initiated by India

BRICS
- Founded: 2006
- Official language: English, Portuguese, Russian, Chinese, Hindi
- BRICS is association of five major emerging national economies: Brazil, Russia, India, China and South Africa

Important International Organizations and their Headquarters

Sl. No.	International Organization	Headquarters	Formation
1.	Asian Infrastructure Investment Bank (AIIB)	Beijing, China	2016
2.	New Development Bank (BRICS Development Bank)	Shanghai, China	2014
3.	Asian Development Bank	Manila, Philippines	1966
4.	United Nations Conference on Trade & Development (UNCTAD)	Geneva, Switzerland	1964
5.	World Economic Forum	Geneva, Switzerland	1971
6.	International Committee of the Red Cross	Geneva, Switzerland	1863
7.	International Atomic Agency	Vienna, Austria	1957
8.	Amnesty International	London, UK	1961
9.	International Olympic Committee	Lausanne, Switzerland	1894
10.	The Federation International de Football Association (FIFA)	Zurich, Switzerland	1904
11.	World Wide Fund for Nature (WWF)	Gland, Switzerland	1961
12.	United Nations Environment Programme	Nairobi, Kenya	1972
13.	Office of the High Commissioner for Human Rights	Geneva, Switzerland	1993
14.	Commonwealth of Independent States	Minsk, Belarus	1991
15.	Gulf Cooperation Council	Riyadh, Saudi Arabia	1981
16.	Organization of Islamic Cooperation	Jeddah, Saudi Arabia	1969
17.	World Trade Organization	Geneva, Switzerland	1995
18.	Islamic Development Bank	Jeddah, Saudi Arabia	1975

Trick to remember headquarters of International Organizations

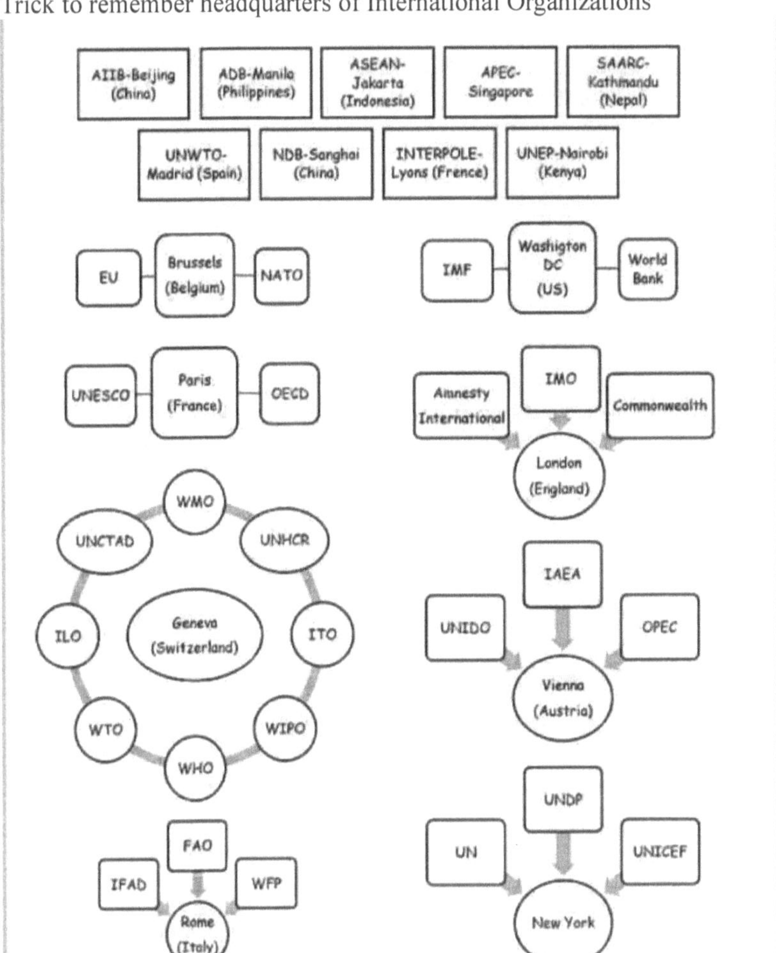

<u>Sports Federations</u>

Sl. No.	Organization Name	Headquarters
1.	International Hockey Federation	Lausanne, Switzerland
2.	Badminton World Federation	Kuala Lumpur, Malaysia
3.	International Tennis Federation	London, UK
4.	Commonwealth Games Federation	London, United Kingdom
5.	International Olympic Committee	Lausanne, Switzerland
6.	International Cricket Council	Dubai, United Arab Emirates
7.	International Federation of Association Football (FIFA)	Zürich, Switzerland
8.	World Chess Federation	Lausanne, Switzerland
9.	Asian Football Confederation	Kuala Lumpur, Malaysia
10.	International Paralympic Committee	Bonn, Germany

<u>International Summits & Conferences</u>

BRICS Summit:
- Established in 2006
- Member Countries: Brazil, Russia, India, China and South Africa
- 16th Summit 2024 – Russia
- 17th Summit 2025 - Brazil

G 20 Summit:
- Established in 2003
- Member Countries: Argentina, Australia, Brazil, Canada, China, France, Germany, India, Indonesia, Italy, Japan, Mexico, Russia, Saudi Arabia, South Africa, South Korea, Turkey, United Kingdom, United States, European Union
- 2023 – India
- 2024 – Brazil
- 2025 – South Africa
- 2026 – United States

G 7 Summit:
- Established on 1975 Member Countries: France, Germany, Italy, Japan, United Kingdom, United States
- 50th 2024 – Italy
- 51st 2025 - Canada

NATO Summit:
- NATO – North Atlantic Treaty Organisation
- Member Countries: 29
- Headquarters: Brussels, Belgium
- 2024 Summit – United States
- 2025 Summit - Netherlands

SAARC Summit:
- SAARC – South Asian Association for Regional Cooperation
- Established- 1985
- Member Countries: Afghanistan, Maldives, Bangladesh, Bhutan, Sri Lanka, Pakistan, India, Nepal
- Headquarters- Kathmandu, Nepal
- 18th SAARC Summit - 2014, Kathmandu
- 19th SAARC Summit - 2016, Pakistan (Cancelled due to Uri Attack)
- 20th SAARC Summit - Pakistan trying to host

ASEAN Summit:
- ASEAN – Association of South East Asian Nation
- Established on 1967
- Member Countries: Brunei, Philippines, Laos, Thailand, Vietnam, Malaysia, Indonesia, Myanmar, Cambodia, Singapore
- 44th & 45th Summit 2024 – Laos
- 46th & 47th Summit 2025 – Malaysia
- 48th & 49th Summit 2026 - Philippines

East Asia Summit (EAS):
- Established on 2005
- Member Countries: Australia, Brunei, Cambodia, China, India, Indonesia, Japan, Laos, Malaysia, Myanmar, New Zealand, Philippines, Russia, Singapore, South Korea, Thailand, United States, Vietnam
- 19th 2024 – Laos
- 20th 2025 - Malaysia

IBSA Summit:
- Established in 2003
- Member Countries: India, Brazil, South Africa
- 1st Summit 2006- Brazil
- 6th Summit 2013 – India, New Delhi (Cancelled)
- 7th Summit 2017 – South Africa

BIMSTEC Summit:
- BIMSTEC- Bay of Bengal Initiative for Multi-sectoral Technical and Economic Cooperation
- Member Countries: Bangladesh, India, Myanmar, Sri Lanka, Thailand, Bhutan, Nepal
- 5th Summit 2022– Colombo, Sri Lanka

CHOGM Meeting:
- CHOGM- Commonwealth Heads of Government Meeting
- CHOGM 2024 – Samoa
- CHOGM 2026 – Antigua and Barbuda

APEC Summit:
- APEC- Asia Pacific Economic Cooperation
- Establishment – 1989
- Headquarters- Singapore
- Member Countries: Australia, Canada, Brunei, Chile, China, Taiwan, Hong Kong, Indonesia, Japan, Korea, Malaysia, Mexico, New Zealand, Peru, Philippines, Russia, Singapore, Thailand, United States, Vietnam
- 2024 Summit – Peru
- 2025 Summit – South Korea
- 2026 Summit - China

UN Climate Change Summit:
- COP 28 Meeting 2023 - Dubai, UAE

(COP - Conference of Parties)
- COP 29 2024 – Ajerbaijan
- COP 30 2025 - Brazil

SCO (Shanghai Cooperation Organisation):
- Headquarters: Beijing, China
- Member Countries: China, Kazakhstan, Kyrgyzstan, Russia, Tajikistan, Uzbekistan, Pakistan, India
- SCO Summit 2023 - New Delhi, India
- SCO Summit 2024 – Kazakhstan
- SCO Summit 2025 - China

Flora & Fauna of India

- The term **flora** is used to denote plants of a particular region or period
- The term **fauna** is used to denote animals of a particular region or period

WILD LIFE

- India has a rich and diversified wildlife. It has approximately 90,000 animal species.
- India is the only country in the world that has both tigers and lions.
- The natural habitat of the Indian lion is the Gir forest in Gujarat. The Gir Forest is the last remaining habitat of the Asiatic lion
- Tigers are found in the forests of Madhya Pradesh, the Sundarbans of West Bengal and the Himalayan region
- Elephants are found in the hot wet forests of Assam, Karnataka and Kerala

Conservation of Forest and Wildlife in India

- The Indian Wildlife (Protection) Act was implemented in 1972, with various provisions for protecting habitats. An all-India list of protected species was also published.
- Project Tiger, Project Rhino, Project Great Indian Bustard and many other eco-developmental projects have been introduced.
- Wildlife projects

1. Hangul project-1970
2. Gir Lion project-1972
3. Project Tiger-1973
4. Crocodile Breeding Project-1974
5. Rhinos Conservation-1987
6. Project Elephant-1992
7. Red panda project-1996
8. Project Snow Leopard-2009

<u>**Biosphere reserves**</u>

- There are 18 biosphere reserves in India

1. **Cold Desert**, Himachal Pradesh
2. **Nanda Devi**, Uttrakhand
3. **Khangchendzonga National Park**, Sikkim
4. **Dehang-Debang**, Arunachal Pradesh
5. **Manas**, Assam
6. **Dibru-Saikhowa**, Assam
7. **Nokrek**, Meghalaya
8. **Panna**, Madhya Pradesh
9. **Pachmarhi**, Madhya Pradesh
10. **Achanakmar-Amarkantak**, Madhya Pradesh-Chhattisgarh
11. **Great Rann of Kachchh,** Gujarat **(Largest Area)**
12. **Similipal**, Odisha
13. **Sundarbans**, West Bengal
14. **Seshachalam Hills**, Andhra Pradesh
15. **Agasthyamala**, Karnataka-Tamil Nadu-Kerala
16. **Nilgiri,** Tamil Nadu-Kerala **(First to be Included)**
17. **Gulf of Mannar**, Tamil Nadu
18. **Great Nicobar**, Andaman & Nicobar Island

- Twelve of the eighteen biosphere of India fall under the list of **Man and Biosphere Programme (MAB) of UNESCO**

1. Nilgiri (First to be included in 2000)
2. Gulf of Mannar
3. Sunderbans
4. Nanda Devi
5. Nokrek
6. Pachmarhi
7. Similipal
8. Achanakmar - Amarkantak
9. Great Nicobar
10. Agasthyamala
11. Khangchendzonga (Added under MAB Programme in 2018)
12. Panna, Madhya Pradesh (Added in 2020)

Mnemonic for MAB BR - **No GS GK iN SAPPNA (No -** Nokrek Biosphere Reserve (BR), **G -** Gulf of Mannar BR, **S -** Simlipal BR, **G -** Great Nicobar BR, **K -** Khangchendzonga BR, **(i)N -** Nilgiri BR, **S -** Sunderbans BR, **A -** Achanakmar-Amarkantak BR, **P -** Panchmarhi BR, **P -** Panna BR, **N -** Nanda Devi BR, **A -** Agasthyamalai BR)

<u>Superlatives</u>

<u>Important Superlatives of India</u>

- The longest Bridge Above Water: **Dhola Sadiya Bridge, Assam (9.15 km.)**
- The largest animal Fair: **Sonepur (Bihar)**
- The largest Auditorium: **Sri Shanmukhananda Hall (Mumbai)**
- The largest Lake (Freshwater): **Wular Lake (J & K)**
- The largest Lake (Salt water): **Chilka Lake (Odisha)** (brackish water lagoon)
- The largest Saltwater Lake (inland) – **Sambhar Lake, Rajasthan**
- The highest Dam: **Tehri dam**
- The largest Desert: **Thar (Rajastan)**
- The largest cave Temple: **Kailash Nath Temple (Ellora, Maharashtra)**
- The largest Zoo: Arignar Anna Zoological Park- **Vandalur Zoo (1300 Acres)**
- The highest peak: **Kangchenjunga (8586m)**
- The longest Tunnel: **Chenani- Nasri tunnel (Syama Prasad Mookerjee Tunnel) (9.2 km)**
- The largest Delta: **Sundarbans (W. Bengal)**
- The State with maximum forest area: **Madhya Pradesh**
- The longest Corridor: **Corridor of Ramanathaswamy Temple of Rameswaram (Tamil Nadu)**
- The highest Waterfall: **Kunchikal Falls (Karnataka)**
- The longest Road: **NH44 (Srinagar to Kanyakumari) (3745 km)**
- The highest Gate way: **Buland Darwaza, Fatehpur Sikri (U.P)**
- The longest River: **The Ganges (2525 km. long)**
- The largest museum: **Imperial Museum or Indian Museum, Kolkata**
- The largest Dome: **Gol Gumbaz, Bijapur (in Karnataka)**
- The Tallest Statue: **Statue of Unity, Narmada District of Gujarat (182m)**
- The largest public sector Bank: **State Bank of India**
- The Biggest Cantilever Bridge: **Rabindra Setu or Howrah Bridge (Kolkatta)**
- The longest Canal: **Indira Gandhi Canal or Rajasthan Canal (Rajasthan)**
- The longest Railway platform: **Hubli Junction railway station, Karnataka** (longest in the World) (1505 m)
- Highest Railway Station – **Ghum, West Bengal**
- Longest Electric Railway Line – **From Delhi to Kolkata via Patna**

- The Biggest Stadium: **Buddh International Circuit (Auto Racing), YuvaBharti (Salt Lake) Stadium Kolkata (football), Narendra Modi Stadium (Cricket)**
- The Longest Passenger Train Route: **Dibrugarh to Kanyakumari**
- The Oldest Church: **St. Thomas Church at palayer, Thrissur (Kerela)**
- The State with longest Coast Line: **Gujarat**
- The Highest Lake: **Cholamu lake (North Sikkim)**
- Longest natural Cave: **Krem Liat Prah, Meghalaya (Also in Asia)**
- The longest river of Southern India: **Godavari**
- The longest Dam: **Hirakud Dam (Orissa)**
- The highest Gallantry Award: **Ashok Chakra (Peacetime), Param Veer Chakra (Wartime)**
- The highest Award: **Bharat Ratna**
- The biggest Church: **Saint Cathedral at old Goa (goa)**
- The Southern Indian State with Longest Costal line: **Andhra Pradesh**
- The Longest Sea Beach: **Marina Beach (Chennai)**
- The Highest Road: **Road at Khardungla, (in Leh –Manali Sector)**
- The largest artificial Lake: **Govind Sagar (Bhakhra Nangal)**
- The deepest River Valley: **Bhagirathi and Alaknanda**
- The largest River without Delta: **Narmada and Tapi**
- The biggest river Island: **Majuli - Brahmputra river (Assam)**
- The largest Planetarium: **Birla Planetarium**
- Largest state in area: **Rajasthan (3,42,239 sq.km)**
- Smallest state in area: **Goa (3,702sq.km)**
- Largest Cave: **Amarnath (J&K)**
- Most Populated City- **Mumbai**
- Biggest Fort- **Red Fort, Delhi**
- First Complete Banking District- **Palakkad, Kerala**
- First IT District- **Palakkad, Kerala**
- Highest Airport- **Kushok Bakula Rimpochhe Airport, Leh airport in Ladakh**
- Largest Library- **National Library, Kolkatta**
- Largest Plateau- **Deccan Plateau**
- Highest Tower – **Kutab Minar at Delhi (88.4 meters high)**
- Largest District – **Kutch district**
- Largest Port – **Jawahar Lal Nehru Port, Mumbai**
- Highest Rainfall – **Cherrapunji (426 inches per annum)**
- Biggest Mosque – **Jama Masjid at Delhi**
- Highest Battle Field - **Siachin Glacier**

List of First in India

- The first President of Republic of India: **Dr. Rajendra Prasad**
- The first Prime Minister of independent India: **Pt. Jawaharlal Nehru**
- The first Chief Justice of Supreme Court of India: **Hiralal J. Kania**
- The first Indian Commander-in-Chief of India: **General Cariappa**
- The first Vice-President of Republic of India: **Dr. Radhakrishnan**
- The first Muslim President of Republic of India: **Dr. Zakir Hussain**
- The first President of India who died while in office: **Dr. Zakir Hussain**
- The first Education Minister independent India: **Abul Kalam Azad**
- The first Home Minister of independent India: **Sardar Vallabh Bhai Patel**
- The first Speaker of the Lok Sabha: **Ganesh Vasudeva Mavalankar**
- First chairman of Rajya Sabha: **Dr. Radhakrishnan**
- The first Chief Election Commissioner of India: **Sukumar Sen**
- The first Prime Minister of India who resigned without completing the full term: **Morarji Desai**
- First Industries and Supplies Minister of Independent India: **Shyama Prasad Mukherjee**
- First Finance Minister of Independent India: **R. K. Shanmukham Chetty**
- First person to resign from the Central Cabinet: **Shyama Prasad Mukherjee**
- The first President of Indian National Congress: **W. C. Banerjee**
- First President of the Indian National Congress of independent India: **Acharya Kripalani**
- The first Muslim President of Indian National Congress: **Badruddin Tayyabji**
- The first Governor General of free India: **Lord Mountbatten**
- The first and the last Indian to be Governor General of free India: **C. Rajgopalachari**
- The first British Governor General of India: **Lord William Bentinck**
- The first British Viceroy of India: **Lord Canning**
- The first Prime Minister of India who did not face the Parliament: **Charan Singh**
- The first Field Marshal of India: **S. H. F. Manekshaw**
- The first Chief of the Army Staff Gen.: **General Maharaj Shri Rajendrasinhji Jadeja**
- The first Indian Air Chief Marshal: **S. Mukherjee**
- First chief of defence staff (CDS) of India: **General Bipin Rawat**
- First Prime Minister from South India: **P. V. Narasimha Rao**
- First Prime Minister born after India's independence: **Shri Narendra Modi**
- First Chairperson of Lokpal of India: **Pinaki Chandra Ghose**

- First Sikh Prime Minister of India: **Manmohan Singh**
- First Sikh President of India: **Giani Zail Singh**
- First Non-Congress Prime Minister to serve a full term: **Atal Bihari Vajpayee**
- The first defence minister of independent India: **Baldev Singh Chokkar**
- The first Indian to join the I.C.S.: **Satyendra Nath Tagore**
- The first Indian member of the Viceroy's executive council: **Satyendra Prasanna Sinha**
- First Non-Congress State government with Majority by a single party: **E. M. S. Namboodiripad of CPI, Kerala**
- The first man who introduced printing press in India: **James Hicky**
- India's first man in space: **Rakesh Sharma**
- The first Indian to cross English Channel: **Mihir Sen**
- First post office opened in India: **Kolkata**
- First disabled friendly bank ATM: **Union Bank of India**
- First expressway of India: **Mumbai - Pune Expressway**
- First state to achieve 100 percent primary education: **Kerala**
- India's first fully organic state: **Sikkim**
- First state to unveil retail policy: **Andhra Pradesh**
- India's first complete digital state: **Kerala**
- First Indian to be appointed as the deputy director-general of programmes (DDP) of the World Health Organization (WHO): **Dr. Soumya Swaminathan**
- India's first satellite: **Aryabhata**
- India's first nuclear reactor: **Apsara**
- First dam in India: **Kallanai Dam**
- The first person to reach Mt. Everest without oxygen: **Sherpa Anga Dorjee**
- The first newspaper in India: **The Bengal Gazette**
- First City to get India's first underwater Metro which is below the flowing Hooghly River: **Kolkata Metro at Kolkata**
- The first Indian Pilot: **J.R.D. Tata**
- First test tube baby of India: **Indira (Baby Harsha)**
- First Indian to climb mount Everest: **Avtar Singh Cheema**
- First 100% visually challenged Indian Foreign Service Officer: **Beno Zephine**
- India's first Wi-Fi city: **Kolkata**
- First Chinese pilgrim to Visit India: **Fa-Hien**
- The first judge of International Court of Justice: **Dr. Nagendra Singh**

<u>Female (First in India)</u>

- The first woman Governor of a State in independent India: **Mrs. Sarojini Naidu**
- The first woman Prime Minister of India: **Mrs. Indira Gandhi**
- The first woman chief justice of a High Court: **Mrs. Leela Seth**
- The first woman Judge in Supreme Court of India: **Mrs. Meera Sahib Fatima Bibi**
- The first woman Ambassador of India: **Miss C. B. Muthamma**
- The first woman Chief Minister of an Indian State: **Mrs. Sucheta Kripalani**
- The first woman President of the United Nations General Assembly: **Mrs. Vijaya Laxmi Pandit**
- The first woman President of the Indian National Congress: **Mrs. Annie Besant**
- First Indian woman president of Indian national congress: **Sarojini Naidu**
- First women President of India: **Pratibha Patil**
- The first woman President of the United Nations General Assembly: **Mrs. Vijaya Laxmi Pandit**
- The first woman I.P.S. Officer: **Mrs. Kiran Bedi**
- The first woman Director General of Police (DGP): **Kanchan Chaudhary Bhattacharya**
- The first woman to receive Bharat Ratna: **Indira Gandhi**
- The first Indian woman to receive Nobel Prize: **Mother Teresa**
- First Indian woman to cross English Channel: **Aarti Saha**
- The first woman to receive Jnanpith Award: **Ashpurna Devi**
- The first woman Lieutenant General: **General Puneeta Arora**
- The first woman pilot in Indian Air Force: **Harita Kaur Dayal**
- The first woman to climb Mount Everest twice: **Santosh Yadav**
- The first woman union minister of India: **Smt Rajkumari Amrit Kaur. (First Health Minister of India)**
- First Indian Woman to become Miss World: **Reita Faria Powell**
- First Indian woman to become miss universe: **Sushmita Sen**
- First Indian Woman to go to space: **Kalpana Chawla**
- First women's court in India: **Malda, West Bengal**
- First woman Speaker of the Lok Sabha: **Meira Kumar**
- First Indian woman who won Ramon Magsaysay award: **Mother Teresa**
- First woman to drive a railway train in India: **Surekha Yadav**
- First woman appointed as the United Nations Civilian Police adviser: **Kiran Bedi**
- First woman Indian Navy pilot: **Sub-lieutenant Shivangi**
- First Indian woman to fly fighter aircraft solo: **Avani Chaturvedi**

- India's first woman external affairs minister: **Sushma Swaraj**
- India's first woman Defence minister: **Indira Gandhi**
- The first woman Speaker of a State Assembly: **Shanno Devi**

Awards and Honours

- The first Indian to win Nobel Prize: **Rabindranath Tagore (also the first Asian to win the prize)**
- The first Indian to get Nobel prize in Physics: **C. V. Raman**
- The first Indian to receive Bharat Ratna award: **Dr. Radhakrishnan, C. Rajagopalachari, C. V. Raman**
- The first person to receive Jnanpith award: **Sri Shankar Kurup**
- The first person to receive Paramveer Chakra: **Major Somnath Sharma**
- The first Indian to receive Magsaysay Award: **Acharya Vinoba Bhave**
- The first person of Indian origin to receive Nobel Prize in Medicine: **Hargovind Khurana**
- The first Indian to receive Stalin Prize: **Saifuddin Kitchlu**
- The first foreigner to receive Bharat Ratna: **Khan Abdul Ghaffar Khan**
- The first Indian to receive Nobel Prize in Economics: **Amartya Sen**
- First Indian to win an Oscar Award: **Bhanu Athaiya**
- The first Indian to win Man Booker Prize: **Arundhati Roy**
- First Indian Woman to become Miss World: **Reita Faria Powell**
- First Indian woman to become miss universe: **Sushmita Sen**
- The First recipient of the Rajiv Gandhi Khel Ratna award: **Chess Grandmaster Viswanathan Anand**

Sport

- The first Indian to swim across the English Channel: **Mihir Sen**
- The first Indian Woman to swim across the English Channel: **Arati Saha**
- First cricketer to score 100 centuries in Test and ODI combined: **Sachin Tendulkar**
- First Indian to hit six sixes in an over in first-class cricket: **Ravi Shastri**
- First Indian woman to score a double hundred in Test cricket: **Mithali Raj**
- First Indian bowler to take hat-trick in ODI: **Chetan Sharma**
- First Indian bowler to take hat-trick in test Cricket: **Harbhajan Singh**
- First Indian to score a T20 century: **Suresh Raina**
- First Captain for Indian ODI cricket team: **Ajit Wadekar**
- First Captain for Indian Test cricket team: **CK Nayudu**
- First chess grandmaster of India: **Mr. Viswanathan Anand**
- First Indian woman wrestler to win an Asian Games gold medal: **Vinesh Phogat**

- First Indian woman badminton player to win an Asian Games medal: **Saina Nehwal**
- The first Indian to win an individual gold medal at the Olympic Games: **Abhinav Bindra**
- India won first gold medal in hockey in **1928** at Amsterdam
- First Indian woman to win Olympic medal: **Karnam Malleswari**
- First Indian woman to win Olympic silver medal: **P.V. Sindhu**
- First Indian Woman to Win an Olympic Medal in Wrestling: **Sakshi Malik**
- First bowler to take all 10 wickets in an innings: **Anil Kumble**

List of First in World

- The first person to reach Mount Everest: **Sir Edmund Hillary & Tenzing Norgay**
- The first man to have climbed Mount Everest Twice: **Nawang Gombu**
- The first President of U.S.A: **George Washington**
- The first Prime Minister of Great Britain: **Robert Walpole**
- The first Governor-General of Pakistan: **Muhammad Ali Jinnah**
- First Prime Minister of Israel: **David Ben-Gurion**
- The first person to reach the North Pole: **Robert Peary**
- The first person to reach the South Pole: **Roald Amundsen**
- The first person to sail around the world: **Ferdinand Magellan**
- The first religion of the world: **Hinduism**
- The first Secretary General of the United Nations: **Trygve Lie**
- The First European who visited China: **Marco Polo**
- The first European to attack India: **Alexander the Great**
- The First US President who visited India: **Dwight D. Eisenhower**
- The first U.S. President to resign Presidency: **Richard Nixon**
- The First person who landed on Moon: **Neil Armstrong**
- The first country to issue paper currency: **China**
- The first country to print book: **China**
- The first country to prepare a constitution: **United States of America**
- The first country to host NAM (Non-Aligned Movement) summit: **Belgrade, Yugoslavia**
- The first person to fly an Aeroplane: **The Wright brothers (Wilbur and Orville Wright)**
- The first country to launch Artificial satellite in the space: **The Soviet Union (First artificial satellite Name: Sputnik I)**
- The first country to host the modern Olympics: **(Athens) Greece in 1896**
- The first man to compile the Encyclopedia: **Aspheosis**
- The first and only player to score test centuries in his first three test matches: **Mohd. Azharuddin (India)**

- The first shuttle to go in space: **Space Shuttle Columbia (NASA)**
- The first spacecraft to reach on Mars: **Viking landers**
- The first city on which the atom bomb was dropped: **Hiroshima (Japan)**
- First man to draw the map of Earth: **Anaximander**
- First man to walk in space: **Alexei Leonov (Soviet cosmonaut)**
- First human being to travel into space: **Yuri Gagarin (USSR)**
- First man to swim across the English Channel: **Matthew Webb**
- First man to win Nobel Prize for Peace: **Jin F Dunant (Switzerland) & Frederic Peiry (France)**
- First man to win Nobel Prize for Physics: **W.K. Roentgen (Germany)**
- First man to win Nobel Prize for Chemistry: **J.H. Wenthoff (Holland)**
- First man to win Nobel Prize for Medicine: **A.E. Worm Behrig (Germany)**
- The first country to commence competitive examination: **China**
- The first country to win the football World cup: **Uruguay**
- The first country to win the cricket World cup: **West Indies**
- The first team to win the Women's Cricket World Cup: **England (1973)**
- The first team to win the Hockey World Cup: **Pakistan**
- The first cricket team to win the T20 World cup: **India (2007)**
- First Asian city to host Olympics: **Tokyo (1964)**
- First woman to cross the Atlantic in a solo flight: **Amelia Earhart**
- First Woman Prime Minister of a country: **Sirimavo Bandaranaike (Sri Lanka)**
- First Woman Prime Minister of any Muslim country: **Benazir Bhutto**
- First Woman Prime Minister of England: **Margaret Thatcher**
- First Woman to climb Mt. Everest: **Junko Tabei (Japan)**
- The first female President of the U.N. General Assembly: **Vijaya Lakshmi Pandit**
- First Woman cosmonaut in space: **Valentina Tereshkova (Soviet cosmonaut)**
- The first woman who reached Antarctica: **Caroline Mikkelsen (Denmark)**
- The first woman who received a Nobel Prize: **Marie Curie (For Physics ,1903)**
- First woman to win an Olympic gold: **Charlotte Cooper (England)**
- First woman to swim across the English Channel: **Gertrude Ederle**
- First woman to win the Man Booker Prize: **Bernice Rubens (for The Elected Member)**
- First woman to walk on space: **Svetlana Savitskaya**
- The first animal to go into space: **Laika**
- The first President of Chinese Republic: **Sun Yat Sen**
- The first Prime Minister of Pakistan: **Liaquat Ali Khan**

Sikkim General Knowledge Question Bank

1. Who was the First Chogyal of Sikkim?
a. Palden Thendup Namgyal
b. Chakdor Namgyal
c. Thutub Namgyal
d. Phuntsog Namgyal
Ans. (d)
The first Chogyal of Sikkim was Phuntsog Namgyal. He ascended the throne and was consecrated as the Chogyal in 1642 at the age of 38. The coronation took place in Yuksom, which later became the capital of Sikkim under his rule. The term "Chogyal" means "righteous ruler" and was conferred upon Sikkim's Buddhist kings during the reign of the Namgyal Monarchy. Interestingly, this lineage was foretold by the patron saint of Sikkim, Guru Rinpoche, when he arrived in the state.

2. Who was Thekong Tek?
a. Bhutia Cheiftain
b. Limboo
c. Lepcha Chieftain (blessed Khye Bhumsa)
d. None
Ans. (c)
In the 17th century, Bhutias and Lepchas (the original ethnic tribals of Sikkim) ceremonially signed a "Treaty of Blood Brotherhood" at a historic site called Kabi Lungchok. This treaty was a symbol of unity and friendship between the two communities. The literal meaning of "Kabi Lungchok" is "stone erected by our blood".
Khye Bumsa represented the Bhutias.
Thekong Tek, the Lepcha Chief, represented the Lepchas.
The signing of this treaty took place at Kabi Lungchok. The site is marked by stone pillars, and life-size statues of the Lepcha and Bhutia "blood-brothers" stand there as a testament to their bond1.
Khye Bumsa and his wife initially faced infertility. Seeking blessings, they traveled to meet Thekong Tek, a revered Lepcha holy man. With his blessings, they had three sons. One of these sons, Phuntsog Namgyal, eventually became the first Chogyal (monarch) of Sikkim.

3. Who was Khye Bumsa?
a. Youngest son of Guru Tashi
b. Son of Thekong Tek
c. Eldest son of Guru Tashi
d. None
Ans. (c)
Guru Tashi, a Bhutia prince, hailed from the Minyak House in Kham, Eastern Tibet.

In the 14th century, Guru Tashi had a divine revelation one night, instructing him to travel south in search of his fortunes.

Accompanied by his five sons, Guru Tashi settled down in the Chumbi Valley in Sikkim.

His eldest son played a remarkable role in the construction of a monastery. When the workers struggled to erect pillars for the monastery, he single-handedly raised one of the pillars.

As a result, he was bestowed with the title "Kheye Bumsa", which translates to "the superior of ten thousand heroes"

4. Where was the first Chogyal of Sikkim crowned and consecrated?

a. Gangtok

b. Yuksom

c. Tumlong

d. Kabi Lungchok

Ans. (b)

The first Chogyal of Sikkim, Phuntsog Namgyal, was crowned at the Narbugang Coronation Throne, which is located near Yuksom.

Following the crowning of Phuntsog Namgyal, the Norbugang Chorten was erected.

The chorten, also known as a stupa, stands as a testament to this historic event. Lama Lhatsun Chempo played a crucial role during the coronation.

The chorten was also the place where Lama Lhatsun Chempo created a time capsule, burying all the gifts received during the occasion.

The benediction and consecration ceremonies performed by the lamas at the Norbugang Chorten lasted for 21 days.

5. Name the Chogyal who shifted capital from Yuksom to Rabdentse in the year 1670?

a. Thutob Namgyal

b. Chagdor Namgyal

c. Phunstok Namygal

d. Tensung Namgyal

Ans. (d)

Phuntsog Namgyal, the first Chogyal or King of Sikkim, was consecrated as king at Yuksom. His son, Tensung Namgyal, succeeded him in 1670, and during his reign, the capital was relocated to Rabdentse.

6. Name the Chogyal who shifted capital from Rabdanste to Tumlong in the year 1814?

a. Thutob Namgyal

b. Chagdor Namgyal

c. Phunstok Namygal

d. Tsudphud Namgyal

Ans. (d)

Tshudpud Namgyal was concerned about Rabdentse's proximity to the Nepalese border and he shifted the capital to Tumlong.

7. Name the Chogyal who shifted capital from Tumlong to Gangtok in the year 1894?

a. Thutob Namgyal
b. Phuntsog Namgyal
c. Tenzing Namgyal
d. Tashi Namgyal

Ans. (a)

Thutob Namgyal shifted the capital of Sikkim from Tumlong to the current capital of Gangtok in 1894.

8. Who was the Last Chogyal of Sikkim?

a. Palden Thondup Namgyal
b. Chagdor Namgyal
c. Thutub Namgyal
d. Tensung Namgyal

Ans. (a)

Palden Thondup Namgyal, the 12th Chogyal was the last Chogyal of Sikkim. He acceded the kingdom of Sikkim to India in 1975 which ended the monarchy.

9. What is the chronological order of Capital of Sikkim from 1st to last (capital).

a. Gangtok, Rabdanste, Tumlung, Yuksom
b. Yuksom, Rabdanste, Gangtok, Tumlong
c. Tumlong, Yuksom, Gangtok, Rabdanste
d. Yuksom, Rabdanste, Tumlong, Gangtok

Ans. (d)

Correct Chronological order of Capitals of Sikkim is Yuksom, Rabdanste, Tumlong, Gangtok.

10. During whose reign, the Bhutanese forces attacked Sikkim and captured the capital Rabdantse for 8 years?

a. Chagdor Namgyal
b. Tensung Namgyal
c. Phuntsog Namgyal
d. Gyurmed Namgyal

Ans. (a)

During the reign of Chagdor Namgyal, the Bhutanese forces launched an attack on Sikkim and captured the capital Rabdentse for a period of eight years.

11. Who designed Lepcha Alphabet?

a. Thutob Namgyal:

b. Tensung Namgyal
c. Phunstok Namygal
d. Chagdor Namgyal
Ans. (d)

The Lepcha script is derived from the Tibetan script and may have been influenced by Burmese writing. According to tradition, it was devised at the beginning of the 18th century by Prince Chakdor Namgyal of the Namgyal dynasty of Sikkim.

12. Name the Chogyal who was killed by his half-sister?
a. Tensung Namgyal
b. Chakdor Namgyal
c. Phunstok Namygal
d. Tsudphud Namgyal
Ans. (b)

Pedi Ongmu conspired with Tibetian doctor to kill Chagdor Namgyal, her half-brother. At that time, King was holidaying in Ralang hot spring.
Ongmu was strangled to death with silken scarf and the doctor was executed at Namchi.

13. Name the half-sister who killed Chogyal Chagdor Namgayl with the help of Tibetan doctor by opening main artery.
a. Rinzing Wangmoo
b. Tashi Ongmoo
c. Pedi Wangmoo
d. Karma Wangmoo
Ans. (c)

Refer previous question.

14. Name the Chogyal who married Limbu Raja daughter.
a. Tensung Namgyal
b. Chagdor Namgyal
c. Phunstok Namygal
d. Tsudphud Namgyal
Ans. (a)

Tensung Namgyal, the second Chogyal, married the daughter of a Limbu chief.

15. Darjeeling was gifted to British East India Company by Sikkim in the year:
a. 1780
b. 1835
c. 1849
d. 1861
Ans. (b)

In **1835**, Tsugphud Namgyal **gifted Darjeeling** to the East India Company for an annual subsidy fee.

16. Two Britishers Dr. Campbell and Dr. Hooker captured by the Sikkimese in the year

a. 1780
b. 1835
c. 1849
d. 1861

Ans. (c)

In the year 1849, Dr. Campbell and Dr. Hooker, both British individuals were captured and imprisoned by the Sikkimese authorities. The hostilities between Britain and Sikkim escalated, eventually leading to the Treaty of Tumlong in 1861, which effectively made Sikkim a British protectorate.

17. Name the Chogyal who ruled for the longest period.

a. Gyurmed Namgyal
b. Thutob Namgya
c. Tsudphud Namgyal
d. Tensung Namgyal

Ans. (c)

Tsugphud Namgyal (Born 1785-Died 1863) (Ruled from 1793 - 1863, 69 years) was the longest serving chogyal of Sikkim.

18. Name the Chogyal who introduced the system of sending one son to the monastery.

a. Gyurmed Namgyal
b. Chagdor Namgyal
c. Tsudphud Namgyal
d. Tensung Namgyal

Ans. (b)

Chagdor Namgyal commanded that the second of every three sons of Bhutia family must be ordained as monk of Pemiongchi Monastery.

19. What were the people called who minted coins for the Sikkim Durbar?

a. Botanist
b. Taksaris
c. Mangpas
d. Chhodu

Ans. (b)

People who minted coins for the Sikkim Durbar were called as Taksaris.

20. Mr.Colman Macaulay visited Sikkim to explore the possibility of a trade route between Sikkim and Tibet in the year

a. 1817
b. 1884

c.   1793

d.   1700

Ans. (b)

In 1884, Colman Patrick Louis Macaulay, an administrator in British India, embarked on a significant mission to explore the feasibility of establishing a trade route between Sikkim and Tibet.

21. First Invasion of Sikkim by Ghurkhas took place in the year

a.   1788

b.   1816

c.   1793

d.   1817

Ans. (a)

In 1788, Gorkha armies launched an invasion of Sikkim, annexing a significant portion of its territories into Nepal. The ensuing conflict between Nepal and the British culminated in the Anglo-Nepalese War (also known as the Anglo-Gurkha War) from 1814 to 1816. Following the defeat of the Nepalese, the Treaty of Sugauli was imposed by the British, resulting in Nepal ceding various territories, including Sikkim (including Darjeeling), Kumaon, Garhwal, and parts of the western Terai region. Additionally, the region between the Mechi and Teesta Rivers was relinquished by Nepal.

In February 1817, as part of the Treaty of Titalia, the British restored the land originally belonging to Sikkim to the Sikkimese Chogyal. However, in 1829, a border dispute emerged between Nepal and Sikkim, prompting Governor General William Bentinck to dispatch two officers, Captain Lloyd and JW Grant, to mediate. During their brief stay in Darjeeling, the officers were enamored with the area and envisioned its potential as a retreat from the tropical climate of India. Impressed by Darjeeling, Captain Lloyd and JW Grant recommended to the Governor General the acquisition of Darjeeling from Sikkim. Subsequent negotiations with the Chogyal led to the British obtaining the area in 1835.

22. Anglo-Nepalese War between British East India Company and Nepal started where Britain formally declared war with the Nepal on

a.   1st Nov.1814

b.   1st Dec.1816

c.   2nd Dec.1793

d.   1st Nov.1817

Ans. (a)

The Anglo-Nepalese War was fought between the Gorkhali army of the Kingdom of Nepal and the British forces of the East India Company from 1st November 1814 to 4 March 1816.

The war ended with the Treaty of Sugauli on March 4, 1816, which was signed between the British East India Company and Nepal. By the treaty, Nepal remained sovereign but became a protectorate and received a British resident till the Nepal–Britain Treaty of 1923. Nepal renounced all claim to the disputed Tarai, and ceded its conquests west of the Kali River and extending to the Sutlej River.

23. Treaty of Sagauli was signed on........ between the East India Company and the King of Nepal following the Anglo-Nepalese War of 1814-16. This allowed Britain to recruit Gurkhas for military service.

a.   4th March 1816
b.   5th July 1811
c.   4th April 1817
d.   6th Dec. 1880

Ans. (a)

Refer previous question.

24. In which year treaty of Titalia signed between Sikkim and British East India Company (EIC):

a.   1817
b.   1780
c.   1793
d.   1700

Ans. (a)

The Treaty of Titalia was signed between the Chogyal (monarch) of Sikkim and the British East India Company (EIC) in February 1817. The treaty was negotiated by Captain Barre Latter and guaranteed the security of Sikkim by the British and returned Sikkimese land annexed by the Nepalese over the centuries. The treaty followed the Anglo-Nepalese War, 1814-1816.

25. In which year, the Nepali Gorkha Army invaded Sikkim, and took Limbuana and the former capital Rabdentse by storm.

a.   1788
b.   1780
c.   1670
d.   1793

Ans. (a)

In 1788, the Gorkha Army from Nepal launched a forceful invasion of Sikkim, seizing Limbuana and the former capital Rabdentse. As a result, the Sikkimese king, Tenzing Namgyal sought refuge in Tibet.

In 1793, the Tenzing Nagyal's son, Tshudpud Namgyal, returned to Sikkim with Chinese assistance to reclaim the throne. Concerned about Rabdentse's proximity to the Nepalese border, he decided to relocate the capital to Tumlong.

26. Kazis were chosen for the first time in Sikkim in the year:

a.   1773
b.   1780
c.   1670
d.   1793

Ans. (a)

Kazis were chosen for the first time in Sikkim in the year 1773 by Chogyal Phuntsog Namgyal.

27. In which year the British clashed with the Tibetans on the Eastern border of Sikkim, Gnathang?
a.   1817
b.   1888
c.   1793
d.   1700
Ans. (b)
The British clashed with the Tibetans on the Eastern border of Sikkim, Gnathang in 1888.

28. Sikkim became a British protectorate by Tumlung Treaty, signed between the Ashley Eden and the Sidkeong Namgyal (son of Tsugphud Namgyal) in the year.
a.   1817
b.   1861
c.   1793
d.   1700
Ans. (b)
The Treaty of Tumlong was signed on 29 February 1861 between the British Empire and the Kingdom of Sikkim. Sir Ashley Eden signed the treaty on behalf of the British Empire, and Sidkeong Namgyal, the Chogyal of Sikkim, signed it on behalf of Sikkim. The treaty secured protection for travelers to Sikkim and guaranteed free trade, thereby making the state a de facto British protectorate.

29. Sikkim became an Indian protectorate in the year
a.   1947
b.   1950
c.   1960
d.   1956
Ans. (b)
In 1950 the Indo-Sikkimese Treaty made Sikkim an Indian protectorate, with India assuming responsibility for the external relations, defense, and strategic communications of Sikkim.

30. Name the Chogyal who was educated in Oxford University.
a.   Gyurmed Namgyal
b.   Sidkeong Tulku
c.   Tsudphud Namgyal
d.   Tensung Namgyal
Ans. (b)
Sidkeong Namgyal was educated in Oxford University.

31. In which year the first bank called Jetmull and Bhojraj was opened in Sikkim?
a.   1800

b.   1700
c.   1899
d.   1900
Ans. (c)
The first bank of Sikkim Jetmul Bhojraj was established in 1899 and very soon it became the Official Bank of the Government of Sikkim and remained functional till 1970s.

32. **Anglo Chinese Convention signed for border between Sikkim and Tibet in the year**
a.   1890
b.   1780
c.   1642
d.   1762
Ans. (a)
The **Anglo-Chinese Convention of 1890**, also known as the **Convention of Calcutta**, was a significant treaty between **Great Britain** and **Qing China**. It demarcated the Sikkim–Tibet border.

33. **Finish Missionaries started primary schools at Khamdong, Sang and Martam in the year**
a.   1880
b.   1780
c.   1642
d.   1762
Ans. (a)
Finish Missionaries started primary schools at Khamdong,Sang and Martam in the year 1880.

34. **Scottish Missionaries started schools at Rhenock, Pachekhani, Pakyong, Damthang, Chakung, Soreng, Turuk in the year**
a.   1884
b.   1780
c.   1642
d.   1762
Ans. (a)
Scottish Missionaries started schools at Rhenock, Pachekhani, Pakyong, Damthang, Chakung, Soreng, Turuk in the year 1884.

35. **John Claude White was appointed as a Political Officer in the North East Indian Kingdom of Sikkim in the year:**
a.   1889
b.   1780
c.   1642
d.   1762
Ans. (a)

John Claude White, a **British civil servant**, held the position of **Political Officer in Sikkim** from **1889 to 1908**. During this period, Sikkim was under British protectorate, and White played a crucial role in managing British India's relations with <u>Tibet</u> and <u>Bhutan</u> as well

As the Political Officer, White had several significant responsibilities:

Sikkim Administration: He served as the **Chairman of the Council** advising Sikkim's Chogyal Thutob Namgyal. Under his guidance, Sikkim's administration was reorganized, land and mineral surveys were conducted, and unused wasteland was developed. Additionally, he established a forestry department and introduced English apple cultivation in the northern towns of Lachung and Lachen.

Sikkim-Tibet Boundary Investigation: Following the **1890 Convention of Calcutta**, which addressed the Sikkim-Tibet boundary and trade relations, White was tasked with investigating the location known as **"Yatung"** in the Chumbi Valley for the establishment of a trade mart. His report highlighted that although the Chinese were friendly, they had no real authority over Tibet, concluding that "China was suzerain over Tibet only in name."

Tibet Expedition: In 1903, Lord Curzon appointed the **Tibet Frontier Commission** under Francis Younghusband. White served as Younghusband's deputy during the **1903-04 British expedition to Tibet**. Although the expedition aimed to settle disputes over the Sikkim-Tibet border, it effectively became a de facto invasion of Tibet. White, the only member permitted to photograph Lhasa's monasteries, played a significant role in this expedition.

Bhutan Exploration: White made five trips to Bhutan and, in 1907, photographed the coronation of Bhutan's first king.

36. **John Claude White introduced Zamindari System, Thikadari System Kalobhari, Jharlangi and Theki-bethi in Sikkim during the in the year:**
a. 1890-1908
b. 1790-1708
c. 1690-1709
d. 1762-1780

Ans. (a)

John Claude White introduced Zamindari System, Thikadari System Kalobhari, Jharlangi and Theki-bethi in Sikkim during his tenure from 1890-1908.

37. **First Population Census conducted in Sikkim before merger to India:**
a. 1891
b. 1780
c. 1642
d. 1762

Ans. (a)

The **first population census** conducted in Sikkim before its merger with India took place in **1891**. According to the British Political Officer's records, Sikkim had a total population of **30,458** individuals. Among them, **11,589** were males, **10,563** were females, and **8,306** were children

38. Forest Department of Sikkim was established in the year:
a.   1907
b.   1809
c.   1910
d.   1909
   Ans. (d)
Forest Department of Sikkim was established in the year 1909.

39. High Court of Sikkim was established in the year:
a.   1975
b.   1960
c.   1963
d.   1979
   Ans. (a)
High Court of Sikkim was established in the year 1975.

40. STNM was established in the year:
a.   1909
b.   1917
c.   1920
d.   1945
   Ans. (b)
The original **Sir Thutob Namgyal Memorial (STNM) Hospital** was established **in 1917** in the heart of Gangtok, Sikkim. However, it has now shifted its premises to a new and impressive 10-storied hospital called the **Sir Thutob Namgyal Memorial Multi-Speciality Hospital (STNM)**, located in Sochaygang, approximately three kilometers away from Gangtok.
Some key points about the new hospital:
Size and Bed Capacity: The STNM Multi-Speciality Hospital boasts a whopping **1,002 beds**, making it the **second largest government hospital in India**, trailing only behind the prestigious **All India Institute of Medical Sciences (AIIMS)** in New Delhi.
Construction and Cost: It took **nine years** and a staggering ₹**1,281 Crore** to build. The hospital is spread across **15 acres** of land, providing ample space for medical facilities and services.
Earthquake-Resistant Design: Considering the region's seismic activity, the hospital's main block has been constructed using **earthquake-resistant materials**. It is designed to withstand tremors measuring up to **8 on the Richter scale**

41. Revenue Order No.1 was introduced by CA Bell in the year:
a.   1909
b.   1917
c.   1910
d.   1907
   Ans. (b)

The **Revenue Order No. 1** was issued by **C.A. Bell**, the Superintendent of Sikkim, on **17th May 1917**.
Purpose and Context:
The order aimed to regulate land rights and management in Sikkim.
It specifically addressed the **Bhutia** and **Lepcha** communities.
Key Provisions:
Restrictions on Land Transactions:
Bhutias and Lepchas were **not allowed** to sell, mortgage, or sublet their lands to anyone other than fellow Bhutias or Lepchas.
Any such transaction required **express sanction** from the Durbar (the royal court) or authorized officers.

42. Paljor Namgyal Girls School established in the year:
a. 1924
b. 1917
c. 1910
d. 1907
Ans. (a)
Paljor Namgyal Girls School was **established in 1924** by the Scottish missionary **Hon'ble Dr. Mary Hepburn Scott**

43. First motor vehicle 'Beatle" arrived in Gangtok in the year:
a. 1924
b. 1917
c. 1910
d. 1907
Ans. (a)
First motor vehicle 'Beatle" arrived in Gangtok in the year 1924.

44. Whitehall inaugurated by J.C. White in the year:
a. 1932
b. 1949
c. 1910
d. 1907
Ans. (a)
Sikkim Whitehall was established in **1932** in memory of **Sir John Claude White,** the first Political Officer of Sikkim

45. Sikkim Nationalised Transport Department was established in year:
a. 1910
b. 1917
c. 1944
d. 1907
Ans. (c)
The **Sikkim Nationalised Transport Department** was established in the year **1955**.

46. Namgyal Institute of Tibetology was established in the year:
a.   1958
b.   1960
c.   1950
d.   1947
Ans. (a)
The foundation stone of the museum was laid by the 14th Dalai Lama on 10 February 1957. On October 1, 1958, Pandit Jawaharlal Nehru, the then Prime Minister of India, inaugurated the Sikkim Research Institute of Tibetology. Sir Tashi Namgyal, the then Maharaja of Sikkim, changed its name into the "Namgyal Research Institute of Tibetology.

47. Sikkim Subject Certificate was issued to Bhutia, Lepcha and Limboo from:
a.   1960
b.   1961
c.   1950
d.   1947
Ans. (b)
Sikkim Subject Certificate was issued to Bhutia, Lepcha and Limboo from 1961 under the Sikkim Subject Regulation Act 1961.

48. State Bank of Sikkim was established in the year:
a.   1947
b.   1960
c.   1950
d.   1968
Ans. (d)
The **State Bank of Sikkim (SBS)** was established in **1968** under the **State Bank of Sikkim Proclamation, 1968**. The bank plays a crucial role in handling both banking services and treasury functions for the **Sikkim State Government**. As an autonomous body wholly owned by the **Government of Sikkim**, it operates independently and is not regulated by the **Reserve Bank of India**.

49. Sikkim became twenty second state of India during the reign of which Chogyal:
a.   Gyurmed Namgyal
b.   Sidkeong Tulku
c.   Palden Thondup Namgyal
d.   Tsudphud Namgyal
Ans. (c)
Sikkim became twenty second state of India in 1975 during the reign of Chogyal Palden Thondup Namgyal.

50. Who was First Dewan of Sikkim?

a.   Gurbachan Singh
b.   Nari Rustomji
c.   Baleshwar Prasad
d.   John S. Lall
 Ans. (d)
John S. Lall was the first Dewan of Sikkim who served from 11 August 1949 –
1954.

51. Name the first Political officer of Sikkim.
a.   John Claude White
b.   Charles Bell
c.   Hopkinson
d.   N.B Menon
 Ans. (a)
The **first political officer of Sikkim** was **John Claude White**, who served
from **1889-1908** appointed by the British-India Government.

52. Name the first Indian Political officer of Sikkim.
a.   Shri Harishwar Dayal
b.   Charles Bell
c.   James Claude White
d.   Hopkinson
 Ans. (a)
The first Indian Political officer of Sikkim was Harishwar Dayal who served from
1948-1952.

**53. What did the 35th Amendment of the Constitution of India passed on 5th
    Sept. 1974?**
a.   Full Fledged State of India
b.   Associated State of India
 Ans. (b)
The 35th Amendment of the Constitution of India, passed on 5th September 1974,
paved the way for Sikkim to be designated as an Associate State within the Indian
Union.
Prior to this amendment, Sikkim was granted the status of a **Protectorate State** of
India.
The historic agreement of **8th May 1973** between the Chogyal (the monarch of
Sikkim), political party leaders representing the people of Sikkim, and the
Government of India laid the groundwork for progressive changes in Sikkim's
governance.
The members of the Sikkim Assembly on **11th May 1974** decided at achieving
a **fully responsible government** in Sikkim and strengthening its relationship with
India.
Government of Sikkim Act, 1974:
The Sikkim Assembly unanimously passed the **Government of Sikkim Bill,
1974.**

The Chogyal promulgated this bill on **4th July 1974**, officially enacting it as the **Government of Sikkim Act, 1974**.

Section 30 of this Act empowered the Government of Sikkim to seek **participation and representation** for the people of Sikkim in India's political institutions.

35th Amendment:

The **Constitution (Thirty-fifth Amendment) Act, 1974** was enacted by the Indian Parliament.

It added a new **Article 2A** to the Constitution, conferring on Sikkim the status of an **Associate State** of the Indian Union.

54. **What did the 36th Amendment of the Constitution of India passed on 16th May 1975?**
a. Full Fledged State of India
b. Associated State of India
   Ans. (a)

The **36th Amendment** of the Indian Constitution, enacted on **May 16, 1975**, made Sikkim a full-fledged state of India.

Background:

The **Sikkim Assembly** unanimously adopted a resolution on **April 10, 1975**.

The resolution noted the **harmful activities of the Chogyal** (the monarch of Sikkim) aimed at undermining the democratic government established under the provisions of the **May 8 Agreement of 1973** and the **Government of Sikkim Act, 1974**.

The Assembly declared that the institution of the Chogyal was abolished, and Sikkim would henceforth be a **constituent unit of India** with a democratic and fully responsible government.

Referendum:

A special **opinion poll** conducted by the Government of Sikkim on **April 14, 1975**, resulted in **59,637 votes in favour** and only **1,496 votes against** the resolution.

The people of Sikkim overwhelmingly supported the decision to abolish the monarchy and integrate Sikkim into the Indian Union.

Outcome:

As a result of this referendum, Sikkim officially became the **22nd state of the Indian Union** on **May 16, 1975**.

The **36th Amendment Act** added Sikkim's name to the **First Schedule** of the Indian Constitution, recognizing it as a full-fledged state within India

55. **When did Sikkim become as Associated State of India?**
a. 5th Sept. 1974
b. 16th May 1974
c. 16th July 1975
d. 4th May 1975
   Ans. (a)

Refer Ques. 53 for details.

56. When did Sikkim become as full- fledged State of India?
a. 5ᵗʰ Sept. 1974
b. 16ᵗʰ May 1975
c. 16ᵗʰ July 1975
d. 4ᵗʰ May 1975
Ans. (b)
Refer Ques.54 for details.

57. Who was the first Governor of Sikkim?
a. Shri P. Shiva Shanker
b. Shri B.B. Lal
c. Shri V Rama Rao
d. Shri B.P Singh
Ans. (b)
The **first governor of Sikkim** was **B. B. Lal**, who assumed office on **May 18, 1975** and served until **January 9, 1981**. Since then, several distinguished individuals have held this position, contributing to the governance and development of the state.
Here's a brief list of the governors of Sikkim:
1. **B. B. Lal**: The inaugural governor, serving from 1975 to 1981.
2. **Homi J. H. Taleyarkhan**: In office from 1981 to 1984.
3. **Kona Prabhakar Rao**: Held the position from 1984 to 1985.
4. **T.V. Rajeswar**: Served as governor from 1985 to 1989.
5. **Radhakrishna Hariram Tahiliani**: His tenure extended from 1990 to 1994.
6. **Chaudhary Randhir Singh**: Governor from 1996 to 2001.
7. **Balmiki Prasad Singh**: Contributed during 2008-2013.
8. **Shriniwas Dadasaheb Patil**: Held office from 2013 to 2018.
9. **Ganga Prasad**: Governor from 2018 to 2023.
10. **Lakshman Acharya**: The current governor, in office since February 13, 2023

58. Name the first Chief Minister of Sikkim.
a. Shri B.B. Gurung
b. Shri Pawan Chamling
c. Shri Nar Bahadur Bhandari
d. Shri L.D. Khangasharpa
Ans. (d)
Chief Ministers of Sikkim:
1. **Kazi Lhendup Dorjee (1975–1979):**
     o   First Chief Minister of Sikkim after its union with India.
     o   Represented the Tashiding constituency.
     o   Affiliated with both the Sikkim National Congress and the Indian National Congress.

2.   **Nar Bahadur Bhandari** (1979–1984):
   - Second Chief Minister.
   - Represented the Soreng constituency.
   - Member of the Sikkim Janata Parishad.
3.   **Bhim Bahadur Gurung** (1984):
   - Briefly held office from May 11, 1984, to May 25, 1984. Shortest term in history of Sikkim.
4.   **Nar Bahadur Bhandari** (1985–1989):
   - Served a second term from March 8, 1985, to November 25, 1989.
   - Associated with the Sikkim Sangram Parishad.
5.   **Sanchaman Limboo** (1994):
   - Fourth Chief Minister of Sikkim.
   - Held office for 179 days from June 17, 1994, to December 12, 1994.
   - Enforced the central act of Other Backward Classes (OBC) in Sikkim.
   - Passed away on November 8, 2020, in Gangtok, Sikkim, India.
6.   **Pawan Kumar Chamling** (1994–2019):
   - Longest-serving Chief Minister.
   - Fifth Chief Minister of Sikkim.
   - Ruled for 24 years.
   - His tenure ended in the 2019 Vidhan Sabha elections.
7.   **Prem Singh Tamang (P. S. Golay)** (since 2019):
   - Current and Sixth Chief Minister.
   - Founder and leader of the Sikkim Krantikari Morcha (SKM).
   - Represents the Poklok-Kamrang constituency in the Sikkim Legislative Assembly.

59. Name the third Chief Minister of Sikkim.
a.   Shri B.B. Gurung
b.   Shri Pawan Chamling
c.   Shri Nar Bahadur Bhandari
d.   Shri Kazi L.D. Khangasharpa
 Ans. (a)
Refer Ques. 58

60. Name the fifth Chief Minister of Sikkim.
a.   Shri B.B. Gurung
b.   Shri Pawan Chamling
c.   Shri Nar Bahadur Bhandari
d.   Shri Kazi L.D. Khangasharpa
 Ans. (b)

Refer Ques. 58

61. The first State Day was observed on:
a.   16ᵗʰ of April, 1973
b.   16ᵗʰ of May, 1974
c.   16ᵗʰ of April, 1975
d.   16ᵗʰ of May, 1975
Ans. (d)
The **Statehood Day of Sikkim** is celebrated annually on **May 16** to commemorate the formation of Sikkim as the **22nd state of India** in **1975**.

62. The President Rule was imposed on May 25,1984. Who was the Governor of Sikkim during that period?
a.   Shri. Homi J.H. Taleyarkhan
b.   Shri P. Shiva Shanker
c.   Shri Bisma Narayan Singh
d.   Shri V. Rama Rao
Ans. (a)
During the period when President's rule was imposed in Sikkim from 25 May 1984 – 8 March 1985, the **Governor** serving was **Homi J. H. Taleyarkhan**

63. The First Lok Sabha member from Sikkim:
a.   Shri Pahal Man Subba
b.   Shri Chatra Bahadur Chettri
c.   Shri Bhim Dahal
d.   Shri Nakul Rai
Ans. (b)
The **first Member of Parliament (MP)** from **Sikkim** was **Chatra Bahadur Chhetri**. He represented the **Sikkim Lok Sabha constituency** during the **1977 general elections** after Sikkim joined the Union in **1975**.

64. The First Rajya Sabha Member from Sikkim:
a.   Shri L.S Saring
b.   Shri O.T. Lepcha
c.   Shri Palden T. Gyatso
d.   Shri Karma Tenzing Tobden
Ans. (a)
The **first Rajya Sabha member from Sikkim** was **Leonard Soloman Saring**, who represented the **Indian National Congress**. His term began on **20th October 1975** and ended on **19th October 1981**

65. Name the person who became the Chief Minister of Sikkim and the MP of Lok Sabha?
a.   Shri Sancha Man Limboo
b.   Shri Pawan Chamling
c.   Shri Bhim Bahal
d.   Shri N.B. Bhandari

Ans. (d)

N.B. Bhandari served as Chief Minister of Sikkim as well as MP of Lok Sabha.

1. **Chief Minister of Sikkim:**
    - o **First Term**: He served as the **Chief Minister of Sikkim** from **18 October 1979** to **11 May 1984**.
    - o **Second Term**: Bhandari held the position of Chief Minister for a second time from **8 March 1985** to **17 June 1994**.
2. **Member of Parliament (MP):**
    - o Bhandari briefly represented the **Sikkim Lok Sabha constituency** as an **independent candidate** in the **8th Lok Sabha** from **1984 to 1985.**

66. Name the first woman member of Lok Sabha (M.P) from Sikkim.

a. Smt. R Ongmoo
b. Smt. D.K. Bhandari
c. Smt. Hem Lata Chettri
d. Smt. Kalawati Subba

Ans. (b)

Dil Kumari Bhandari was the first women MP of Lok Sabha from Sikkim. Dil Kumari was elected as a Member of Parliament from Sikkim twice from May 1985 to 27 November 1989 and from 20 June 1991 to 10 May 1996.

67. Name the first woman MLA of Sikkim.

a. Smt. D.K. Bhandari
b. Smt. Hem Lata Chettri
c. Smt. Kalawati Subba
d. Smt. Nimthit Lepcha

Ans. (b)

The first woman Member of the Legislative Assembly (MLA) from Sikkim was **Hemlata Chhetri (Khatiwada)**. She won the election from the **Geyzing** assembly constituency in **1974** and played a significant role in the **1973** pro-democracy movement.

68. Name the First Speaker of the State Legislative Assembly of Sikkim.

a. Shri Chatur Singh Rai
b. Smt. Kalawati Subba
c. Shri K.T. Gyaltsen
d. Shri D N Thakarpa

Ans. (a)

The first Speaker of the Sikkim Legislative Assembly was Shri C.S. Roy. His tenure lasted from 1974-1979.

69. Name the First Women Speaker of the State Legislative Assembly of Sikkim.

a. Smt. D.K. Bhandari

b.   Smt. Hem Lata Chettri
c.   Smt. Kalawati Subba
d.   Smt. Nimthit Lepcha
Ans. (c)
the First Women Speaker of the State Legislative Assembly of Sikkim was Kalawati Subba. Her tenure was from 1999-2004.

70. Name the First Deputy Speaker of State Legislative Assembly of Sikkim
a.   Shri Chatur Singh Rai
b.   Shri Lal Bdr. Basnet
c.   Shri R.C Paudyal.
d.   Shri D N Thakarpa
Ans. (c)
Shri R.C. Poudyal was the first Deputy Speaker of Sikkim Legislative Assembly from 1975 to 1977.

71. The First President of India to Visit Sikkim:
a.   Dr. Rajendra Prasad
b.   Dr. Sarvepalli Radhakrishnan
c.   Dr. Zakir Hussain
d.   Shri Neelam Sanjeeva Reddy
Ans. (d)
Neelam Sanjeeva Reddy was the first President of India to visit Sikkim in 1979.

72. The Angel of Mercy "Mother Teresa" visited Sikkim on:
a.   17th Feb 1976
b.   9th April 1975
c.   23rd July 1975
d.   30th Aug 1975
Ans. (a)
Mother Teresa visited Sikkim on 17th Feb 1976. Mother Teresa received several honors, the 1962 Ramon Magsaysay Peace Prize, the 1979 Nobel Peace Prize and the Bharat Ratna in 1980.

73. Chogyal Palden Thondup Namgyal passed away in New York City on:
a.   17th Feb. 1976
b.   23rd July 1975
c.   15th Oct. 1982
d.   29th Jan. 1982
Ans. (d)
Chogyal Palden Thondup Namgyal, the 12th and last king of the Kingdom of Sikkim, died on January 29, 1982, at the Memorial Sloan Kettering Cancer Center in New York City, United States. He was 58 years old at the time of his passing. Upon his death, 31 members of the State Legislative Assembly offered khadas to the Chogyal as a mark of respect.

74. First Helicopter service between Bagdogra and Gangtok inaugurated on:
a.   1st May 1982
b.   16th May 1975
c.   4th May 1984
d.   12th Dec.1994
  Ans. (a)
First Helicopter service between Bagdogra and Gangtok was inaugurated on 1st May 1982.

75. When was Nepali Language included in the Eighth Schedule of Indian Constitution?
a.   Sept. 1990
b.   Oct 1993
c.   Aug 1992
d.   Jan 1994
  Ans. (c)
The inclusion of the **Nepali language** in the **Eighth Schedule** of the **Indian Constitution** occurred in Aug **1992** through the **Seventy-First Amendment.**

76. Name the first recipient of Padma Vibhushan Award from Sikkim.
a.   Shri Bhaichung Bhutia
b.   Palden Thondup Namgyal
c.   Kazi Lendup Dorjee Khangsharpa
d.   Pawan Kumar Chamling
  Ans. (c)
L D Kazi was the first recipient of Padma Vibhushan from Sikkim. He was honoured in 2003.

77. What is the Literacy rate of Sikkim as per 2011 census?
a.   68.8%
b.   70%
c.   82.20%
d.   90%
  Ans. (c)
Literacy Rate in Sikkim as per 2011 census is 82.2%.

78. What is the population of Sikkim as per 2011 census?
a.   5,40,493
b.   6,10,577
c.   5,68,073
d.   6,71,760
  Ans. (b)
Population of Sikkim as per 2011 census is 610,577. Out of this, there are 323,070 males and 287,507 females. Sikkim's population constitutes 0.05 percent of India's total population in 2011. The state covers a total area of 7,096 square

kilometers and witnessed a population growth of 12.89 percent during the decade from 2001 to 2011.

79. The First Chief Secretary of Sikkim:
a.   Shri K.C. Pradhan
b.   Shri S.W. Tenzing
c.   Shri T.D Densepa
d.   Shri P.K. Pradhan
Ans. (c)
The first Chief Secretary of Sikkim was Tashi Densapa. He held this position during the period when Sikkim was still a kingdom, before it became the 22nd state of India following a referendum in 1975.

80. The First Chief Justice of Sikkim High Court:
a.   Justic M.M. Singh Gujral
b.   Justice M.L. Shrimal
c.   Justice J.K. Mohanty
d.   Justice R.N. Sacher
Ans. (a)
Justice Man Mohan Singh Gujral (7 May 1976 – 14 March 1983) was the first Chief Justice of the Sikkim High Court.

81. Who was the First Election Commissioner of Sikkim?
a.   Shri R.N. Sengupta
b.   Shri B.B. Lal
c.   Shri R.K Kapoor
d.   Shri Ravi Telang
Ans. (a)
First Election Commissioner of Sikkim was R.N. Sengupta.

82. What is the total area of Sikkim?
a.   7100 sq km
b.   8043 sq km
c.   9064 sq km
d.   7096 sq km
Ans. (d)
The total area of Sikkim is 7096 sq km.

83. What is the male: female ratio as per 2011 census?
a.   1000:990
b.   1000:890
c.   1000:800
d.   1000:900
Ans. (b)
The average sex ratio (which considers all age groups) in Sikkim was 890 females per 1000 males.

84. What is the male literacy rate as per 2011 census?
a.   86.55%
b.   80.20%
c.   68.25%
d.   90.21%
Ans. (a)
As per the 2011 Census,
The overall literacy rate in Sikkim is 81.42%. This is higher than the national average of 72.98% for India. Specifically:
Male Literacy: 86.55%
Female Literacy: 75.61%

85. What is the female literacy rate as per 2011 census?
a.   75.61%
b.   87.29%
c.   78.45%
d.   63.12%
Ans. (a)
Refer Ques 84.

86. What is the average population density of Sikkim as per 2011 census?
a.   234 person per sq. km
b.   86 person per sq. km
c.   300 person per sq. km
d.   450 person per sq. km
Ans. (b)
Average population density of Sikkim as per 2011 census is 86 people per sq. km.

87. In which district the Lonak valley is located?
a.   Gangtok
b.   Gyalshing
c.   Mangan
d.   Namchi
Ans. (c)
The Lhonak Valley, also known as Muguthang Valley, is situated in the Mangan District of Sikkim. It lies near the village of Muguthang and is close to the famous Chopta Valley. This high-altitude valley stands at an elevation of 14,850 feet and is characterized by its trans-Himalayan grasslands, boggy marshes, glacial lakes, barren scree slopes, and glaciers

88. Name the source of Rangit River.
a.   Rathong Glacier
b.   Zemu Glacier:
c.   Lonak Glacier
d.   Talung Glacier

Ans. (a)

Rangit River emanates from a glacial lake near the Rathong Glacier in West Sikkim.

89. Name of source of Teesta River.

a. Rathong Glacier
b. Pauhunri Glacier
c. Lonak Glacier
d. Talung Glacier

Ans. (b)

The Teesta River originates from the Teesta Khangtse Glacier, situated at an elevation of approximately 5,280 meters (17,700 feet) in the North Sikkim district of the Indian state of Sikkim. This glacier lies at the base of the Pauhunri peak (7,056 meters). The river then flows through the entire state of Sikkim in a north-south direction for around 175 kilometers before entering the plains of West Bengal. From there, it continues its journey, eventually merging with the Brahmaputra River in Bangladesh after crossing the border through the Rangpur division. The Teesta drains an area of 12,540 square kilometers.

90. Name the Eastern Tibet-Sikkim Border Pass.

a. Nathula & Jelepla Pass
b. Chiwabhanjang Pass
c. Chorten La Pass
d. Bamcha La Pass

Ans. (a)

Nathula & Jelepla Pass are the Eastern Tibet-Sikkim Border Pass.

    1. **Nathu La Pass**:

Elevation: 4,310 meters (14,140 feet).

Location: It lies in the Dongkya Range of the Himalayas.

Connects: The pass links China's Yadong County in Tibet with the Indian state of Sikkim.

Significance: Nathu La has historical importance as a trade route and a cultural exchange point between the two regions.

Name Interpretation:

Traditionally, it is interpreted as the "whistling pass" or more commonly as the "listening ears pass".

The Chinese government explains it as a place where "snow is deepest and the wind strongest".

According to some interpretations, it means "flat ground from where the hill features gradually rise to right and left".

Tourism and Trade:

The reopening of Nathu La in 2006 provided an alternative route for the pilgrimage to Mount Kailash and Lake Manasarovar.

It was expected to boost the economy of the region by facilitating growing Sino-Indian trade.

However, trade is limited to specific goods and specific days due to weather conditions, including heavy snowfall, restricting border trade to around 7 to 8 months.

2. Jelepla Pass

Elevation: Approximately **4,390 meters (14,390 feet)**.

Location: It lies in the **Dongkya Range** of the **Himalayas**.

Connects: Jelep La serves as a crucial link between Sikkim (India) and the Tibet Autonomous Region (China).

91. Name the Western Nepal-Sikkim Border Pass.

a. Nathula & Jelepla Pass

b. Chiwabhanjang Pass

c. Chorten La Pass

d. Bamcha La Pass

Ans. (b)

Chiwabhanjang Pass is the Western Nepal-Sikkim Border Pass.

Elevation: Approximately **3,139 meters (10,299 feet)** above sea level.

92. Which is the highest pass in Sikkim

a. Nathu-La

b. Chorten La

c. Dongkha La

d. Bantang La

Ans. (c)

Dongkha La pass is the highest pass in Sikkim. Located at North Sikkim, it is at an altitude of **18,156.2 feet or 5,534.0 meters** above the sea level. It connects Sikkim with Tibet.

93. When was the State Planning Commission set up in Sikkim?

a. 8th May 2001

b. 16th May 2006

c. 22nd March 1977

d. 12th Dec 1994

Ans. (a)

State Planning Commission was set up in Sikkim in 8th May 2001.

94. In which year was Sikkim included as an eighth member of North East Council?

a. 2008

b. 2002

c. 2009

d. 2004

Ans. (b)

Sikkim was added as the eighth member of the North-East Council (NEC) in the year 2002. Prior to this, the NEC consisted of seven states: Arunachal Pradesh, Assam, Manipur, Meghalaya, Mizoram, Nagaland, and Tripura. With Sikkim's inclusion, the council expanded its representation to include all eight states of the North Eastern Region. The NEC plays a crucial role in coordinating and promoting development activities in the region.

95. In which year were Limboo and Tamang communities included in the list of Schedule tribe?
a. 2003
b. 2004
c. 2000
d. 2006
Ans. (a)
The Limboo and Tamang communities were officially declared as Scheduled Tribes by the Government of India in the year 2003.

96. On which date Silk Route via Nathu-La reopened after 44 years?
a. 6th July 2006
b. 7th May 2008
c. 13th Feb. 2005
d. 10th July 2004
Ans. (a)
The historic Silk Route via Nathu-La reopened after 44 years of closure on July 6, 2006. This strategic pass was once part of the flourishing Silk route connecting ancient China with India.

97. The oldest Monastery of Sikkim:
a. Dubdi Monastery
b. Enchey Monastery
c. Tashiding Monastery
d. Rumtek Monastery
Ans. (a)
The oldest monastery in Sikkim is the Dubdi Monastery, also known locally as Yuksom Monastery. It was established in 1701 by Chagdor Namgyal, the then King of Sikkim.
Location: Dubdi Monastery is situated near Yuksom, in the Geyzing district.
Hermit's Cell: It was also known as the Hermit's Cell, named after its ascetic founder Lhatsun **Namkha Jigme**. Lhatsun Namkha Jigme, along with two other lamas from Tibet, met at Norbugang near Yuksom and crowned Phuntsog Namgyal as the first King or Chogyal of Sikkim in 1642.
Literal Meaning: The local name "Dubdi" translates to "the retreat".
History and Founding:
Dubdi Monastery is central to the history of Sikkim as it is closely linked to the founding of the State of Sikkim at Yuksom in the middle of the 17th century by Lhetsum Chenpo and his two associate lamas.
Chenpo's green image is enshrined in the Dubdi monastery, commemorating the founding of the Kingdom of Sikkim. It is the only monastery surviving out of the four built at that time.

Architecture:
The monastery was established during the reign of Chagdor Namgyal and features an elaborately painted interior area.

Images of divinities, saints, and other symbols, along with a collection of manuscripts and texts, are housed within the monastery.

The statues of the three lamas responsible for establishing Yuksom are also installed here

98. What is the latitude and longitude of Sikkim?
a. Latitude of 28 degrees North and longitude of 90 degrees East.
b. Latitude of 30 degrees North and longitude of 70 degrees East.
c. Latitude of 27 degrees North and longitude of 88 degrees East.
d. Latitude of 32 degrees North and longitude of 88 degrees East

Ans. (c)

The **latitude** of Sikkim, is approximately **27.532972** N, and the **longitude** is around **88.512218** E.

99. When was Nepali recognised as an official language and included in the Eight Schedule of the Constitution?
a. 71st Constitutional Amendment, 1992
b. 73rd Constitution Amendment, 1992
c. 74th Constitution Amendment, 1992
d. 86th Constitution Amendment, 2002

Ans. (a)

Nepali was recognised as an official language and included in the Eight Schedule of the Constitution via 71st Constitutional Amendment, 1992.

100. When was Sangha seat created in Sikkim?
a. The Royal Proclamation of 1958
b. The Royal Proclamation of 1960
c. The Royal Proclamation of 1963
d. The Royal Proclamation of 1953

Ans. (a)

The Sangha Assembly constituency in Sikkim was established in 1958 by a royal proclamation. This decision came after requests from the monastery associations to the Chogyal, the monarch of Sikkim at the time. The Sangha seat is reserved for the Buddhist monastic community (Sangha) of Sikkim. Only Buddhist monks and nuns, registered with the 111 recognized monasteries in the state, are eligible to contest and cast their votes for this Assembly seat

101. Himalayan range separating Sikkim from Nepal:
a. Singalila Range
b. Chola/Dongkhya Range
c. Pangola Range
d. None of above

Ans. (a)

Singalila Range separates Sikkim from Nepal in the West.

102. Himalayan range separating Sikkim from Tibet and Bhutan in the east:
a.   Singalila Range
b.   Chola/Dongkhya Range
c.   Pangola Range
d.   None of above
 Ans. (b)
Chola/ Dongkhya Range separates Sikkim from Tibet and Bhutan in the east.

103. Himalayan range separating Sikkim from Bhutan:
a.   Singalila Range
b.   Chola/Dongkhya Range
c.   Pangola Range
d.   None of above
 Ans. (c)
Pangola Range separates Sikkim from Bhutan.

104. Who was the founder of Nyingma Sect?
a.   Dalai Lama
b.   Gautam Buddha
c.   Guru Padmasambva
d.   Tshongkhapa
 Ans. (c)
Padmasambhava, also known as Guru Rinpoche, is the revered founder of
the **Nyingma tradition**, which is the oldest school of Tibetan Buddhism.

105. Where is the festival of Bhumchu held?
a.   Enchey Monastary
b.   Rumtek Monastary
c.   Tashiding Monastary
d.   Lingdum Monastary
 Ans. (c)
The Bhumchu festival is celebrated at the Tashiding Monastery in West Sikkim,
India. This sacred Buddhist festival takes place on the 15th day of the first month
of the lunar calendar, which corresponds to the months of February/March on the
Gregorian calendar.

106. What is the village head man in North Sikkim known as?
a.   Yebba
b.   Mangpa
c.   Chhodu
d.   Pipon
 Ans. (d)

Village head man in North Sikkim is known as Pipon.

107. Name the State Bird of Sikkim?
a.   Blood Pheasant
b.   Peacock
c.   Munal
d.   Pigeon
 Ans. (a)
Blood Pheasant is the State Bird of Sikkim.

108. Name the State Flower of Sikkim?
a.   Alpine Flower
b.   Dendrobium nobile
c.   Rhododendron
d.   Lillies
 Ans. (b)
Noble Orchid or Dendrobium nobile is the State Flower of Sikkim.

109. Name the Rhododendron Sanctuary near Yumthang:
a.   Fambong Lha
b.   Shinba
c.   Maenam
d.   Tendong
 Ans. (b)
Shinba Rhododendron Sanctuary is located near Yumthang.

110. Where does rivers Lachen chu and Lachung chu meet?
a.   Lachung
b.   Lachen
c.   Kabi
d.   Chungthang
 Ans. (d)
The **Lachen Chu** and **Lachung Chu** rivers converge at **Chungthang**.

111. What was the title given to the person who minted coins of Sikkim?
a.   Taksari
b.   Choddu
c.   Chogyal
d.   Thudop
 Ans. (a)
People who minted coins of Sikkim were known as Taksaris.

112. Name the Sanctuary in East Sikkim opposite Gangtok on the Rumtek Hill.
a.   Shingba Wild Life Sanctuary
b.   Maenam Wild Life Sanctuary

c.   Fambong Wild Life Sanctuary

d.   Rhododendron Sanctuary

Ans. (c)

Fambong Lho Wildlife Sanctuary spans an area of **51 square kilometers** and is located on Rumtek Hill, opposite Gangtok.

113. When was the referendum seeking the full merger of Sikkim with Indian held?

a.   July 1992

b.   May 1975

c.   January 1947

d.   April 1975

Ans. (d)

The referendum seeking the full merger of Sikkim with India was held on 14 April 1975. During this referendum, the Sikkim State Council, with the support of Indian Prime Minister Indira Gandhi, unanimously voted to abolish the monarchy and merge with India in order to obtain full Indian statehood. Approximately 97.55% of voters approved the proposal, resulting in Sikkim becoming an Indian state123. The historic decision marked the end of Sikkim's monarchy and its integration into the Indian Union.

114. First State of Indian to launch free Hepatitis "B" vaccination:

a.   Sikkim

b.   West Bengal

c.   Kerala

d.   Bihar

Ans. (a)

Sikkim became the first Indian State to launch free Hepatitis B vaccination on 2001.

115. Sikkim Organic Mission launched on:

a.   1St Jan. 2015

b.   18th Jan. 2015

c.   15th August 2010

d.   21St May 2014

Ans. (c)

In 15th August 2010, the Sikkim Organic Mission was launched with a visionary goal: to convert 75,000 hectares of land into organic farming practices.

116. When did Prime Minister Shri. Narendra Modi declared Sikkim a fully Organic State?

a.   1st Jan.2015

b.   18th Jan.2015

c.   18th Jan.2016

d.   21st May.2014

Ans. (c)

In 18th **January 2016**, Prime Minister **Narendra Modi** officially declared **Sikkim** as **India's first fully organic state**.

117.Sikkim was declared as the first Nirmal Rajya in:
a. 2007
b. 2002
c. 2005
d. 2008
Ans. (d)
Sikkim holds the distinction of being India's first Open Defecation Free (ODF) state. This remarkable achievement was recognized when the Indian Government bestowed upon Sikkim the prestigious "Nirmal Rajya" award in 2008

118.Sikkim achieved open defecation free status in the year:
a. 2016
b. 2002
c. 2005
d. 2008
Ans. (d)
Sikkim was declared an open defecation free state in 2008, 6 years before the Swachh Bharat Abhiyan was launched.

119.Sikkim Public Service Commission was established in the year:
a. 1977
b. 1978
c. 1980
d. 1981
Ans. (b)
Sikkim Public Service Commission was established in the year 1978.

120.Tashi Namgyal Academy was founded by the late Sir Tashi Namgyal in the year:
a. 1926
b. 1927
c. 1928
d. 1929
Ans. (a)
Tashi Namgyal Academy was founded in **1926 by** Late Sir Tashi Namgyal.

121. In which year, the Indo-Sikkimese Treaty was signed?
a. 1954
b. 1947
c. 1975
d. 1950
Ans. (d)

The **Indo-Sikkimese Treaty** was signed in **1950**. This treaty marked a significant moment in history, as it made **Sikkim** an **Indian protectorate**.

122. **Largest Buddhist Monastery in Sikkim:**
a.   Enchey Monastery
b.   Pemayangtse Monastery
c.   Rumtek Monastery
d.   Ralang Monastery
 Ans. (c)
The **largest Buddhist monastery in Sikkim** is the **Rumtek Monastery**, also known as the **Dharma Chakra Centre**.

123. **Temi Tea Garden, which is the only tea garden in Sikkim is located in**
a.   Namchi District
b.   Gangtok District
c.   Soreng District
d.   Pakyong District
 Ans. (a)
Temi Tea Garden is located in Namchi District.

124. **The national research centre of orchids (ICAR) is located in which state of India**
a.   Assam
b.   Manipur
c.   Himachal Pradesh
d.   Sikkim
 Ans. (d)
The **National Research Centre for Orchids (NRCO)**, established by the **Indian Council of Agricultural Research (ICAR)**, is situated in **Sikkim**.

125. **What percentage of Sikkim is covered by Khangchendzonga National Park?**
a.   25%
b.   33%
c.   45%
d.   20%
 Ans. (a)
Khangchendzonga National Park, also known as the **Kanchenjunga Biosphere Reserve**, is a remarkable natural treasure located in **Sikkim, India**. It was inscribed as a **UNESCO World Heritage Site** in July 2016, making it India's first "Mixed Heritage" site.
1.   The park spans an impressive 849.5 square kilometers (328.0 square miles).
2.   It stretches across the Mangan district and Gyalshing district in Sikkim.
3.   The elevation within the park varies from 1,829 meters (6,001 feet) to over 8,550 meters (28,050 feet)

4. It covers approximately 25% of the State of Sikkim

126. Which one is the largest district of Sikkim by area wise?
a. Gyalshing District
b. Gangtok District
c. Mangan District
d. Soreng District

Ans. (c)

The largest district in Sikkim by area is Mangan. It covers an area of 4,226 square kilometers.

127. Who was the first chancellor of Sikkim University?
a. Mahindra P. Lama
b. Avinash Khare
c. M.S Swaminathan
d. Tanka Bahadur Subba

Ans. (c)

The first Chancellor of Sikkim University was M. S. Swaminathan. Additionally, Mahendra P. Lama served as the first Vice Chancellor of the university. Sikkim University began its journey in 2008 with four departments, including Social System and Anthropology, Peace and Conflict Studies and Management, International Relations/Politics, and Microbiology.

128. By which amendment Sikkim become a full State of India?
a. 35th Amendment
b. 36th Amendment
c. 30th Amendment
d. 32nd Amendment

Ans. (b)

On 14th April 1975, a referendum was held, and approximately 97% of the population voted in favor of merging with India.

On 26th April 1975, the Indian Parliament approved the 36th Constitutional Amendment, officially making Sikkim a state of India.

The amendment was ratified by the President on 15th May, and Sikkim was formally admitted to the Union of India on 16th May 1975.

129. How many Rajya Sabha seats does Sikkim have?
a. One
b. Two
c. Three
d. None of the above

Ans. (a)

Sikkim has One Rajya Sabha seat.

130. How many Lok Sabha seats does Sikkim have?
a. One

b.   Two

c.   Three

d.   None of the above

 Ans. (a)

Sikkim has One Lok Sabha seat.

131.In which year Sikkim became a princely state of British India?

a.   1890

b.   1817

c.   1820

d.   1857

 Ans. (a)

Sikkim became a princely state of British India in 1890.

132.What is the Motto of the Sikkim?

a.   Satyameva Jayate

b.   Kanglasha

c.   Kham-Sum-Wangdu

d.   Jai Sikkim

 Ans. (c)

The motto of Sikkim is Kham-sum-wangdu, which means the "conqueror of the three realms.

133.Which flower is on the Emblem of Sikkim?

a.   Marigold

b.   Lotus

c.   Rose

d.   Sunflower

 Ans. (b)

Lotus which is a Symbol of Purity & Administrative Power.

134.Which National Highway connects Gangtok with Siliguri?

a.   NH5

b.   NH8

c.   NH10

d.   NH14

 Ans. (c)

The **National Highway 10 (NH 10),** formerly known as **NH 31A,** is the road that links **Gangtok** in **Sikkim** with **Siliguri** in **West Bengal.**

135.What is the State Animal of Sikkim?

a.   Snow Lion

b.   Red Panda

c.   Himalayan Thar

d.   Deer

 Ans. (b)

The Red panda is the state animal of Sikkim.

136.What is the State Bird of Sikkim?

a. Indian roller
b. Emerald dove
c. Blood Pheasant
d. Himalayan monal

Ans. (c)

The Blood Pheasant is the state bird of Sikkim.

137.In which district the Yumthang Valley of Flowers Sanctuary is located?

a. Mangan District
b. Gyalshing District
c. Soreng District
d. Namchi District

Ans. (a)

Yumthang Valley of Flowers Sanctuary is located in Mangan District.

138.Who was Sikkim's last sovereign King?

a. Tashi Namgyal
b. Palden Thondup Namgyal
c. Phuntsog Namgyal
d. Thutob Namgyal

Ans. (b)

Palden Thondup Namgyal was the last sovereign king of Sikkim. He ruled from 1963 until 1975.

139.Total number of members in the Sikkim Legislative Assembly is

a. 30
b. 32
c. 34
d. 33

Ans. (b)

Total number of members in the Sikkim Legislative Assembly is 32.

140.Phurchachu, Yumthang, Borang, Ralang, Taram-chu and Yumey Samdong in Sikkim are famous?

a. Lakes
b. Rivers
c. Mountains
d. Hot Springs

Ans. (d)

Phurchachu, Yumthang, Borang, Ralang, Taram-chu and Yumey Samdong in Sikkim are famous Hot Springs.

141.How many Presidents' Rule was implemented in Sikkim?

a. 2

b.   1
c.   3
d.   5
 Ans. (a)
Presidents Rule In Sikkim:
1) 18 Aug 1979 – 17 Oct 1979
2) 25 May 1984 – 8 Mar 1985

142. When was Sikkim High Court was established?
a.   12th January 1974
b.   28th December 1974
c.   16th May 1975
d.   20th June 1975
 Ans. (c)
Sikkim High Court was established on 16th May 1975.

143. Who is the longest-serving Chief Minister of Sikkim?
a.   L.D Kazi
b.   Nar Bahadur Bhandari
c.   Pawan Chamling
d.   Sanchaman Limboo
 Ans. (c)
Pawan Kumar Chamling (24 Years, 166 Days) is the longest serving CM of Sikkim as well as of India.

144. Chu-Faat, Zo-Mal-Lok, Tendong Lo Rum Faat, Kinchum-Chu-Bomsa are folk dances of?
a.   Bhutias
b.   Lepchas
c.   Nepalese
d.   None of these
 Ans. (b)
Chu-Faat, Zo-Mal-Lok, Tendong Lo Rum Faat, Kinchum-Chu-Bomsa are folk dances of Lepchas.

145. The monks of _____ Monastery are entitled to the title "ta-tshang"
a.   Tashiding
b.   Dubdi
c.   Pemayangtse
d.   All of the above
 Ans. (c)
Monks of Pemayangtse Monastery are entitled to the title "ta-tshang".

146. What does the name "Sikkim" mean?
a.   Su: Old & Khyim: Palace
b.   Su: Palace & Khyim: King

c. Su: New & Khyim: Palace
d. Su: People & Khyim: Palace
 Ans. (c)
The word "su" means "new", and "khyim" means "palace" or "house". Thus,
Sikkim could be interpreted as the "new palace" or "new house"
In Tibetan, **Sikkim** is known as **"Drenjong"**, which translates to the **"valley of
rice"**.
The Bhutias call it **"Beyul Demazong"**, which means **"the hidden valley of
rice"**.

147. What is the Tibetan name for Sikkim?
a. Bhutia
b. Demazong
c. Drenjong
d. Indrakil
 Ans. (c)
Note - The Tibetan name for Sikkim is **Drenjong** which means "valley of rice ",
while the Bhutias call it Beyul Demazong, which means "the hidden valley of
rice".

**148. Which festival symbolizes the birth, Enlightenment and achieving
    nirvana by Lord Buddha?**
a. Pang Lhabsol
b. Saga Dawa
c. Loosong
d. Drukpa Teschi
 Ans. (b)
Saga Dawa festival indicates the three events that happened on the same day in
the life of Buddha. On this same day, Lord Buddha took birth, attained
enlightenment and passed away attaining Nirvana.
Saga Dawa is observed on the **full moon day of the fourth month** in the
Buddhist calendar.

149. What is the Bhutia name for Sikkim?
a. Nirmahal
b. Beyul Demazong
c. Drenjong
d. Indrakil
 Ans. (b)
The Bhutias call Sikkim **"Beyul Demazong"**, which means **"the hidden valley
of rice"**.

**150. Which district is "Budha Park" also known as "Tathagata Tsal" located
    in Sikkim?**
a. Namchi District
b. Soreng District

c.   Gangtok District
d.   Gyalshing District
 Ans. (a)
"Budha Park" also known as "Tathagata Tsal" is located in Ravangla in Namchi District.

151. What is the height of the statue of Buddha in the Buddha Park of Ravangla?
a.   15 m
b.   20 m
c.   25 m
d.   40 m
 Ans. (d)
The height of the statue of Buddha in the Buddha Park of Ravangla is 40 meters.

152. What is the Sikkim's highest Civilian Award?
a.   Sikkim Shrama Vir
b.   Sikkim Ratna
c.   Sikkim Shrama Shree/Devi
d.   Sikkim Shrama Vishista Award
 Ans. (b)
Sikkim Ratna is the Sikkim's highest Civilian Award.

153. Which Article in Indian constitution give special provision for Sikkim?
a.   370A
b.   371F
c.   371E
d.   371C
 Ans. (b)
Article 371F of the **Indian Constitution** provides **special provisions** with respect to the state of **Sikkim.**

154. Which year did the British East India Company attack Nepal through Sikkim which resulted in the Gurkha War?
a.   1804
b.   1814
c.   1824
d.   1841
 Ans. (b)
The **Anglo-Nepalese War**, also known as the **Gurkha War**, took place between **1 November 1814** and **4 March 1816**. It was fought between the **Gorkhali army of the Kingdom of Nepal** (present-day Nepal) and the **British forces of the East India Company** (EIC, present-day India).
The war eventually ended with the signing of the **<u>Sugauli Treaty</u>** in **<u>1816</u>**, which resulted in the cession of some Nepalese-controlled territory to the East India Company

155. **Where did the holy men consecrate the first Chogyal of Sikkim?**
a.   Rabdentse
b.   Yuksom
c.   Tumlong
d.   Gangtok
Ans. (b)
The first Chogyal of Sikkim, Phuntsog Namgyal, was consecrated in Yuksom in 1642. During the coronation, three revered lamas arrived from different directions—north, west, and south—to perform the sacred ceremony. The title "Chogyal" means "righteous ruler" and was bestowed upon Sikkim's Buddhist kings during the reign of the Namgyal Monarchy. The patron saint of Sikkim, Guru Rinpoche, had foretold the rule of these kings when he arrived in the state.

156. **Who became the third Chief Minister of Sikkim from 11 May until 24 May 1984, the shortest term in history of Sikkim?**
a.   N.B Bhandari
b.   B.B. Gurung
c.   Sanchaman Limboo
d.   L.D. Kazi
Ans. (b)
Bhim Bahadur Gurung (11 October 1929 – 28 March 2022) was the third Chief Minister of Sikkim. He held office from 11 May until 24 May 1984, the shortest term in the history of Sikkim.

157. **Who led delegation of British to Sikkim in 1884 to explore a trade route with Tibet through the Lachen valley?**
a.   Claude White
b.   Long Fellow
c.   Colman Macauley
d.   Claude McDonald
Ans. (c)
In 1884, the British sent a delegation led by Colman Macaulay, the financial Secretary to the Bengal Government of British India, to Sikkim. Their mission was to explore the possibility of establishing a trade route with Tibet through the Lachen valley.

158. **What is the meaning of the term "Nathu La"?**
a.   Nathu: Buddhist & La: Pass
b.   Nathu: Listening Ears & La: Pass
c.   Nathu: Trading & La: Pass
d.   Nathu: Pilgrimage & La: Pass
Ans. (b)
Nathu means "listening ears" and La means "pass" in Tibetan.

159. **The Pakyong airport was inaugurated in:**

a. 2016
b. 2017
c. 2019
d. 2018

Ans. (d)

The **Pakyong Airport**, located in Sikkim, India, was **inaugurated on 24th September 2018** by **Prime Minister Narendra Modi**. Following its inauguration, **commercial flight operations** commenced on **4th October 2018**. This airport holds several distinctions:

- It is the **first greenfield airport** constructed in Northeast India.
- It stands as the **100th operational airport** in India.
- At an elevation of **4,646 feet (1,416 meters)**, it ranks among the **five highest airports** in the country.
- Major media outlets worldwide have praised its engineering and described it as one of the **most scenic airports** globally.

160. At what height is the Nathu La Pass located?

a. 6310 m
b. 5310 m
c. 4310 m
d. 3310 m

Ans. (c)

Nathu La Pass is located at a height of 4310 meters.

161. Which festival is celebrated to pay homage to Mount Kanchenjunga in Sikkim?

a. Pang Lhabsol
b. Bhumchu
c. Tendong Lho Rum Faat
d. Sakewa

Ans. (a)

The festival celebrated to pay homage to **Mount Kanchenjunga** in **Sikkim** is called **Pang Lhabsol**.

162. When did the last major earthquake strike in Sikkim that had a magnitude of 6.9MW killing 60+ people?

a. 2015
b. 2013
c. 2010
d. 2011

Ans. (d)

The last major earthquake in Sikkim occurred on September 18, 2011. It was a powerful quake with a moment magnitude of 6.9. The epicenter was located within the Kanchenjunga Conservation Area, near the border of Nepal and the

Indian state of Sikkim. The earthquake struck at 18:10 IST and was felt across northeastern India, Nepal, Bhutan, Bangladesh, and southern Tibet. Tragically, at least 111 people lost their lives due to this seismic event.

163. Sisekpa Tumyen is a festival celebrated by which community
a. Limboo
b. Tamang
c. Gurung
d. Rai
Ans. (a)
Sisekpa Tumyen is one of the major festivals of the Limboos and is celebrated in the month of Sise:kla (mid-July) every year. It marks the end of drought, famine, hardship and misery and heralds the beginning of prosperity and good luck. It coincides with "sawaney sankrati" of the Nepali.

164. What is the height of the highest lake "Gurudongmar Lake" in Sikkim?
a. 6430 m
b. 5430 m
c. 5500 m
d. 4560 m
Ans. (b)
Gurudongmar Lake is one of the highest lakes in the world and in India, at an elevation of **5,430 m (17,800 ft).**

165. What is the Height of Lake Tsomgo?
a. 1753 m
b. 2750 m
c. 3753 m
d. 4210 m
Ans. (c)
Tsomgo Lake is located at an elevation of **3,753 m (12,313 ft).**

166. Which flower is locally known as "Christmas Flower" in Sikkim?
a. Aphyllorchis
b. Poinsettia
c. Corallorhiza
d. Sardinia
Ans. (b)
Poinsettia is known as Christmas flower in Sikkim.

167. What is the IATA of Pakyong Airport?
a. PYG
b. PKG
c. PAG
d. PNG
Ans. (a)

International Air Transport Association (IATA) code for Pakyong Airport is PYG.

168. At what height is the Pakyong Airport located?
a.   5600 ft
b.   4646 ft
c.   4200 ft
d.   3450 ft
 Ans. (b)
Pakyong Airport sits at an elevation of **4,646 feet (1,416 meters)**, making it one of the **five highest airports in India.**

169. In which census year did Sikkim record a negative percentage in their growing population?
a.   1981
b.   1961
c.   1921
d.   2001
 Ans. (c)
Sikkim recorded a negative population growth in 1921.

170. What was the Per Annum Growth Rate of Sikkim in 2011 as compared to 2001?
a.   +4.19%
b.   +2.01%
c.   +1.22%
d.   +0.89%
 Ans. (c)
Note – Sikkim Population in 2001 Census = 5.41 lakh
In 2011 Census = 6.11 lakh
So, growth in population in 10 years = 70 thousand or about 12.9%
So annual growth rate during this period = 12.9/10 = 1.29%. Closest option is (c).

171. Which district is the Kirateshwar Mahadev Temple located in?
a.   Gyalshing District
b.   Soreng District
c.   Namchi District
d.   Pakyong District
 Ans. (a)
Kirateshwar Mahadev Temple is located in Legship in Geyzing District.

172. Which monastery is popularly known as Dharma Chakra Centre?
a.   Dubdi Monastery
b.   Pemayangtse Monastery
c.   Rumtek Monastery
d.   Rinchenpong Monastery
 Ans. (c)

Rumtek Monastery is known as the Dharma Chalkra Centre.

173. What is the rank of Sikkim on Per Capita alcohol consumption amongst all Indian states?

a. First
b. Fourth
c. Third
d. Fifth

Ans. (c)

According to the 2021 National Family Health Survey-5 (NFHS-5) data, alcohol consumption patterns in India can be summarized as follows:

For men, states with high alcohol consumption rates include 1. Arunachal Pradesh (52%), 2. Telangana (43%), 3. Sikkim (39.8%), then followed by Manipur, Goa, and Jharkhand.

Among women, Sikkim has the second-highest alcohol consumption rate among women (16%), after Arunachal Pradesh (24%)

174. Which monthly magazine was the first news outlet of Sikkim?

a) Prajashakti
b) Kanchenjunga
c) Samay Dainik
d) Sikkim Express

Ans. (b)

Note – Kashiraj Pradhan started the first monthly news Magazine, 'Kanchenjunga' in 1957. He is known as the *Father of Sikkimese journalism.*

175. Where is the National Institute of Technology, Sikkim located?

a. Pelling
b. Yuskom
c. Gangtok
d. Ravangla

Ans. (d)

As of Dec 2023, NIT, Sikkim is being operated from a temporary campus at Ravangla, South Sikkim. Permanent campus of NIT Sikkim is coming up at Khamdong, Sikkim.

176. In which year was the Sikkim University established?

a. 2009
b. 2005
c. 1997
d. 2007

Ans. (d)

Sikkim University is a central university established in 2007. Its temporary campus is scattered around Gangtok as of Dec 2023. The permanent campus is being built at Yangang in Namchi district, about 56 kilometres (35 mi) from

Gangtok. Its first chancellor was M. S. Swaminathan; Mahendra P. Lama was the first vice chancellor.

177. Who was the first Vice-Chancellor of Sikkim University?
a.   M.S Swaminathan
b.   Avinash Khare
c.   Mahendra P. Lama
d.   R.K. Majumdar
Ans. (c)
Mahendra P. Lama was the first vice chancellor of Sikkim University.

178. Which supercomputer does NIT Sikkim hold at their campus?
a.   PARAM ISHAN
b.   PARAM Yuva
c.   PARAM Kanchenjunga
d.   PARAM Brahma
Ans. (c)
Named after the third-highest mountain in the world, Mt. Kangchenjunga, the supercomputer is the fruit of the collaboration between Pune-based Centre for Development of Advanced Computing (C-DAC) and the NIT Sikkim.

179. Which is the oldest University in Sikkim?
a.   Sikkim University
b.   SRM University
c.   Sikkim Manipal University
d.   ICFAI University
Ans. (c)
Establishment Dates:
Sikkim Manipal University – 1995
ICFAI University - 2004
Sikkim University – 2007
SRM University – 2013

180. How many languages are recognized by the Government of Sikkim?
a.   Nine
b.   Five
c.   Four
d.   Twelve
Ans. (d)
Official Languages of Sikkim are English, Nepali, Sikkimese (Bhutia) and Lepcha **(4)**. Additional official languages include Gurung, Limbu, Magar, Mukhia, Newari, Rai, Sherpa and Tamang for the purpose of preservation of culture and tradition in the state. (12 languages).

181. The Teesta River of Sikkim joins with which River in Bangladesh?
a.   Hoogly River

b. Mahanadi River
c. Jamuna River
d. Ganges
Ans. (c)
Teesta River joins the River Brahmaputra, Known as Jamuna in Bangladesh.

182. Which is the largest Buddhist Monastery in Sikkim?
a. Rumtek Monastery
b. Enchey Monastery
c. Pemayangtse Monastery
d. Tashiding Monastery
Ans. (a)
The largest monastery in Sikkim is the Rumtek Monastery, also known as the Dharma Chakra Centre. It serves as the seat of the Kagyu order of Tibetan Buddhism and is home to approximately 500 monks.

183. Which is the main tributary of the Teesta River?
a. Lachung River
b. Rangpo River
c. Rangeet River
d. Rani Khola
Ans. (c)
Largest tributary of the river Teesta is the River Rangit.

184. Which is the Left Tributary of Teesta River?
a. Zemu Chhu
b. Rangyong Chhu
c. Rangit River
d. Rangpo River
Ans. (d)
Left and right bank tributaries that contribute to the Teesta River:
Left Bank Tributaries:
- Lachung Chu
- Chakung Chhu
- Dik Chhu
- Rani Khola
- Rangpo Chhu

Right Bank Tributaries:
- Zemu Chhu
- Rangyong Chhu
- Rangit River

185. Which is the Right Tributary of Teesta River?
a. Dik Chhu
b. Rani Khola
c. Lachung Chu
d. Rangyong Chhu
Ans. (d) Refer previous question.

186. **What is the meaning of the term "Lachen"?**
a.   Big Pass
b.   Bypass
c.   Big Lake
d.   Big Valley
 Ans. (a)
The name Lachen means "Big Pass".

187. **Which is the highest Dam in Sikkim?**
a.   Rangit III Dam
b.   Rangpo Dam
c.   Rongli Dam
d.   Teesta -V Dam
 Ans. (d)
With a height of 86.8m, Teesta-V Dam located in Dikchu, Gangtok District is the highest dam in Sikkim.

188. **The festival "Losar" is celebrated as?**
a.   Flower Festival
b.   Farmer's New Year
c.   Tibetan New Year
d.   Birth of Gautama Buddha
 Ans. (c)
Losar, also known as Tibetan New Year, marks the beginning of the lunisolar Tibetan calendar. It typically falls in February or March in the Gregorian calendar.

189. **When is Sikkim State Day celebrated?**
a.   16th November
b.   16th March
c.   16th April
d.   16th May
 Ans. (d)
Sikkim State Day is celebrated on May 16 which commemorates the formation of Sikkim as the 22nd state of India on May 16, 1975.

190. **Where is India's highest ATM located?**
a.   Yumthang Valley
b.   Nathu La Pass
c.   Tsomgo Lake
d.   Lachung
 Ans. (b)
India's highest ATM is located at an altitude of 14,300 feet in the Kupup region, near the Nathu La Pass in Sikkim. This ATM was inaugurated by the Union Bank of India.

191. **What is the meaning of "Saga Dawa"?**

a. Lights
b. Sacred Pot
c. New Year
d. Fourth Month
Ans. (d)
Saga Dawa or the Triple Blessed Festival is an auspicious month for the Sikkimese Buddhists with prayers held throughout the month in various monasteries.
On the full moon of this 4th month of the Tibetan calendar (April / May month) [celebrated as Buddha Purnima in the rest of India] is the main celebration.
Believed that on this day the **Buddha was born, attained Enlightenment and achieved nirvana.**

192. When was "Fambong Lho Wildlife Sanctuary" established?
a. 1974
b. 1977
c. 1987
d. 1984
Ans. (d)
Fambong Lho Wildlife Sanctuary, established in 1984 is a 51 km² (20 sq mi) large wildlife sanctuary in the Gangtok district, Sikkim and is located about 20 kilometres from Gangtok.

193. Who are said to be the original inhabitants of Sikkim?
a. Lepchas
b. Bhutias
c. Nepalese
d. Limbus
Ans. (a)
The Lepchas are believed to be the original inhabitants of Sikkim.

194. Name the Folk Wind Instrument made of Bamboo found in Sikkim?
a. Khomok
b. Panthong Palit
c. Sarenda
d. Ektara
Ans. (b)
The Panthong Palit is a horizontal flute, approximately one meter long, made entirely from bamboo. It is closed at the blowing end and features a blowing hole a few centimeters down from the closed end. Additionally, there are four finger holes along its length. This traditional instrument is commonly used in folk and traditional musical forms, especially during wedding celebrations in Sikkim.

195. What is the elevation of Lachung?
a. 4,700 m
b. 5,800 m

c.   2,900 m
d.   1,900 m
 Ans. (c)
Lachung is at an elevation of about 9,600 feet (2,900 m).

196. What is found in Yumthang Valley?
a.   Flower Sanctuary
b.   Animal Sanctuary
c.   River
d.   Mosque
 Ans. (a)
Yumthang Valley, also known as the Sikkim Valley of Flowers, is a natural sanctuary in North Sikkim, India. Situated at an elevation of 3,564 meters (11,693 feet), it features a river, hot springs, yaks, and rolling meadows, all surrounded by the Himalayan mountains.

197. Where is Zero Point located in Sikkim?
a.   Thangu Valley
b.   Nathang Valley
c.   Yumthang Valley
d.   Chopta Valley
 Ans. (c)
Zero Point Sikkim, also known as Yumesamdong, is a scenic spot located near Yumthang Valley in North Sikkim. It is situated at an altitude of 15,300 feet above mean sea level. The place is often called "Zero Point" because there is no motorable road after this place and the visitors are not permitted to go beyond this point due to its proximity to the Chinese border.

198. Who is the first Chairperson of Lokayukta of Sikkim?
a.   Justice Anand Prakash Subba
b.   Justice Pratap Krishna Lohara
c.   Justice Vinod Kumar Sharma
d.   Justice Uma Nath Singh
 Ans. (a)
The first Chairperson of Lokayukta in Sikkim is Justice A. P. Subba. He is a former Judge of the High Court of Sikkim and was appointed to this position on July 10, 2020.

199. When was Sikkim Lokayukta formed?
a.   2011
b.   2012
c.   2013
d.   2014
 Ans. (b)

The Sikkim Lokayukta was first formed under the Sikkim Lokayukta and Deputy Lokayukta Act-2012 and approved by the President of India. The passage of the Lokpal and Lokayukta's Act, 2013 in Parliament became law on January 16, 2014, which required each state to appoint its Lokayukta within a year.

Lokayukta is an official appointed by the government to represent the interests of the public. It serves as an anti-corruption authority or ombudsman. Specifically, the Lokayukta investigates allegations of corruption and maladministration against public servants. Its primary function is to ensure speedy redressal of public grievances. The establishment of Lokayukta is governed by the Lokpal and Lokayukta Act, 2013, which aims to inquire into corruption-related complaints against certain public functionaries.

200. Who was the first recipient of the Padma Bhushan Award from Sikkim?
a. Nawang Gurung
b. Sonam Gyatso
c. Triguna Tshering
d. Krishna Tshering Lepcha
Ans. (b)
Sonam Gyatso won the Padma Bhusan in 1965. He was the second Indian man, the seventeenth man in world and the first person from Sikkim to summit Mount Everest the highest peak in the world.

201. Who was the first recipient of the Padma Shri Award from Sikkim?
a. Sonam Wangyal
b. Gadul Singh Lama
c. Sonam Gyatso
d. Phu Dorjee
Ans. (c)
Sonam Gyatso won the Padma Shri in 1962. He was the second Indian man, the seventeenth man in world and the first person from Sikkim to summit Mount Everest the highest peak in the world.

202. In which year did Baichung Bhutia receive the Padma Shri Award?
a. 2007
b. 2008
c. 2009
d. 2010
Ans. (b)
Bhaichung Bhutia won the Padma Shri in 2008. He is also a recipient of Arjuna Award in 1998.

203. How many countries border Sikkim?
a. 1 Country
b. 2 Countries
c. 3 Countries
d. 4 Countries

Ans. (c)
Countries Bordering Sikkim Are:
1) China (North & Northeast)
2) Nepal (West)
3) Bhutan (East)

204. When was Khangchendzonga National Park inscribed in the UNESCO World Heritage Sites?
a.   2014
b.   2015
c.   2016
d.   2017

Ans. (c)
Khangchendzonga National Park was inscribed to the UNESCO World Heritage Sites list in July 2016, becoming India's first "Mixed Heritage" site

205. Which is the smallest district of Sikkim?
a.   Pakyong District
b.   Namchi District
c.   Geyzing District
d.   Soreng District

Ans. (d)
Soreng District is the smallest district in Sikkim with an area of 293.2 sq km. Prior to creation of 6 districts, Namchi District was the smallest with an area of 750 sq km.

206. What is the State Tree of Sikkim?
a.   Burans
b.   White teak
c.   Deodar
d.   Rhododendron

Ans. (d)
Rhododendron is the State Tree of Sikkim.

207. When did the Government of Sikkim formally create 2 new districts and rename the existing 4 districts?
a.   9 Dec 2019
b.   9 Dec 2020
c.   9 Dec 2021
d.   9 Dec 2022

Ans. (c)
The Sikkim government recently created two new districts, Soreng (formerly part of West Sikkim) and Pakyong (formerly part of East Sikkim), bringing the total number of districts in the state from four to six. This change was implemented through the Sikkim Reorganization of Districts Act 2021, which received the assent of the Governor on December 9, 2021.

208. When is Khas Diwas Celebrated?

a. 25 January

b. 26 February

c. 31 November

d. 19 August

Ans. (b)

Chief Minister of Sikkim Prem Singh Tamang announced on 26 Feb 2025 that Khas Diwas will be celebrated on 26th February every year.

www.ingramcontent.com/pod-product-compliance
Lightning Source LLC
Chambersburg PA
CBHW062226150726
47991CB00006B/2456